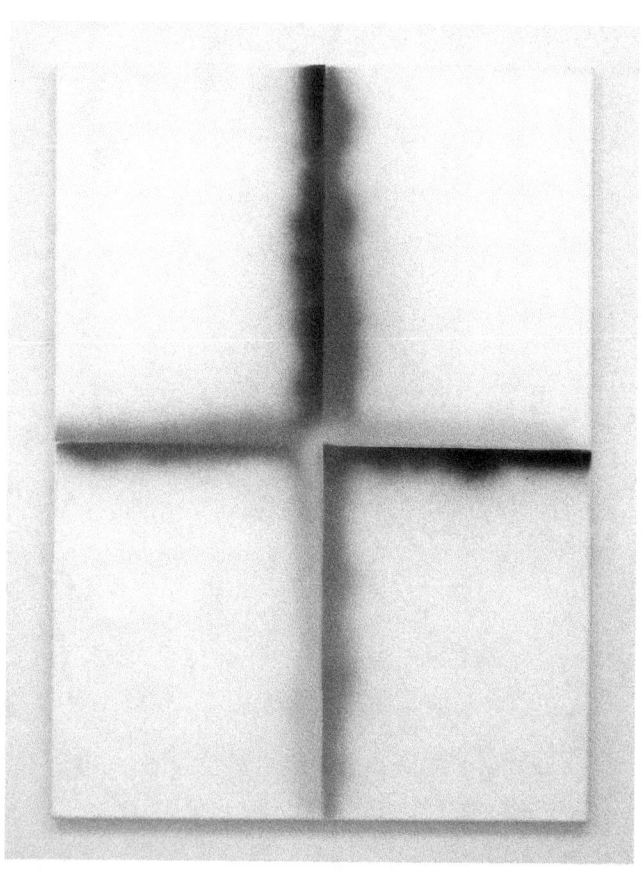

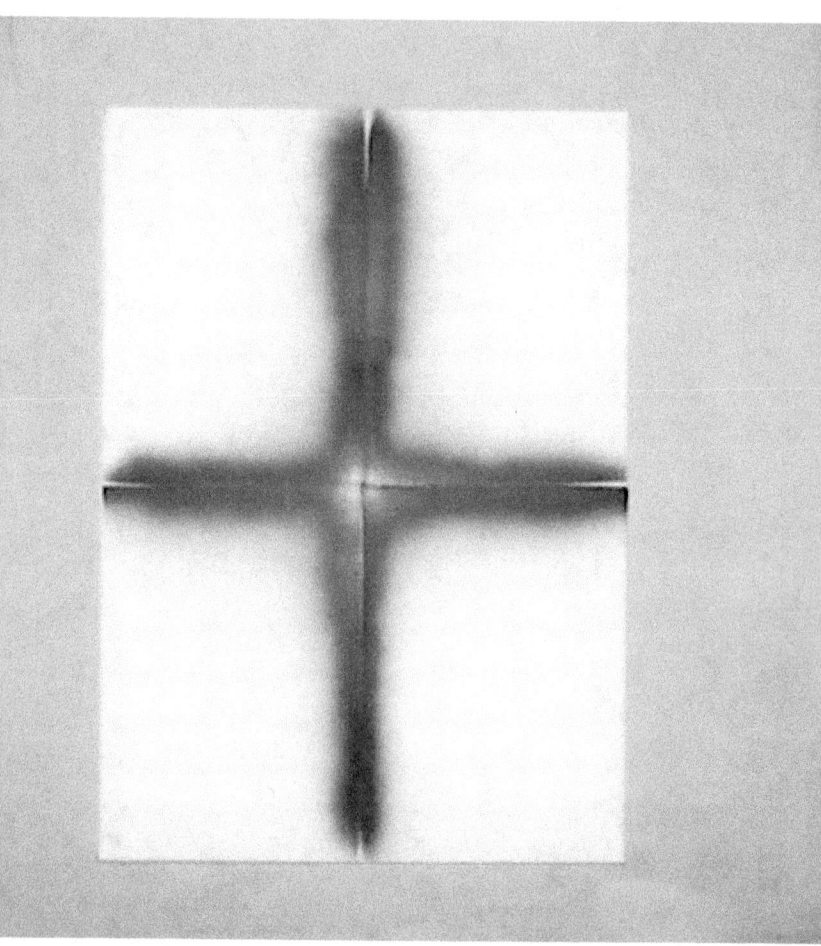

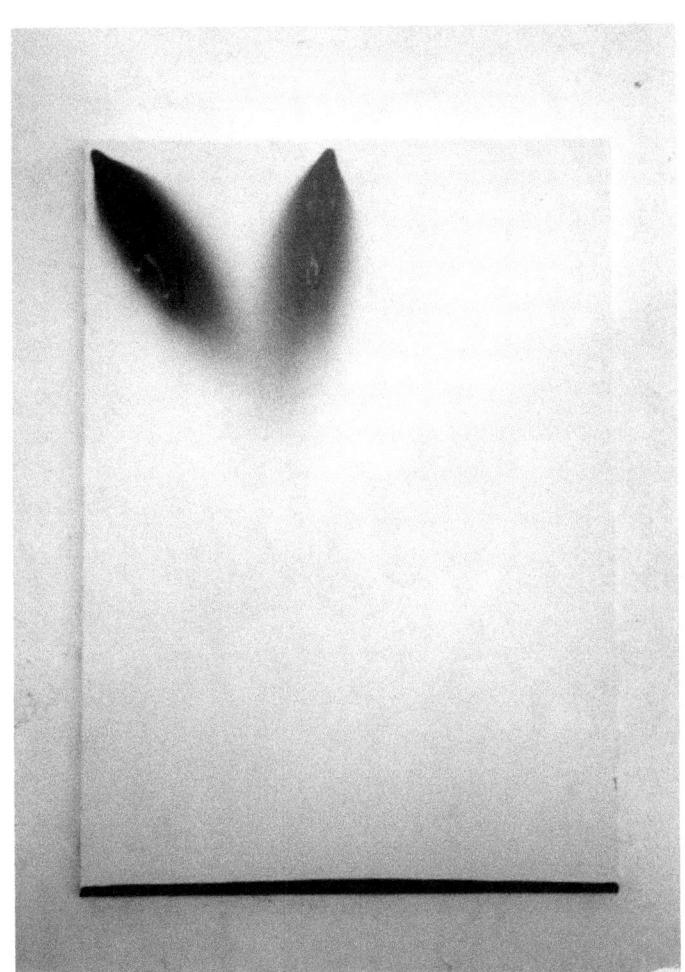

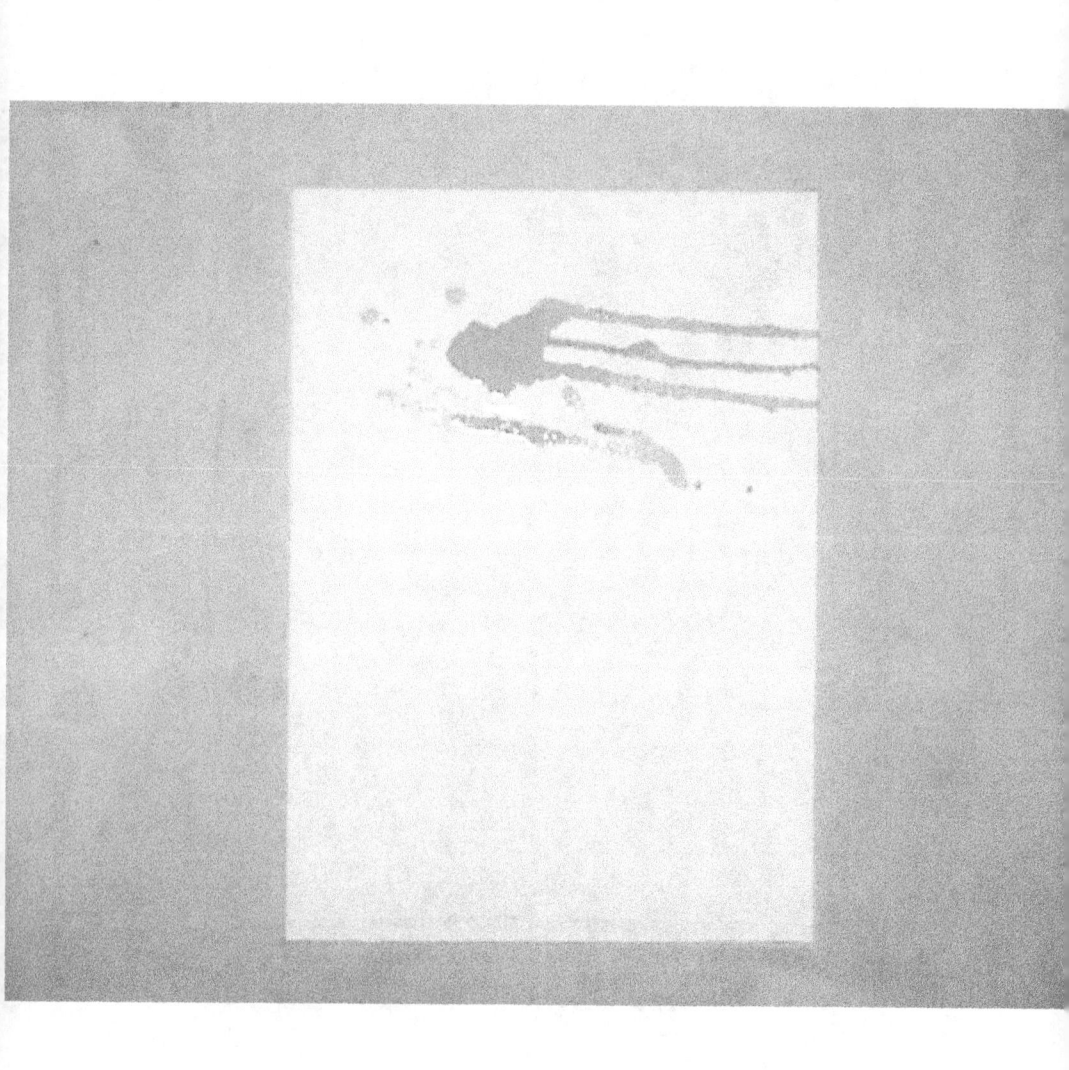

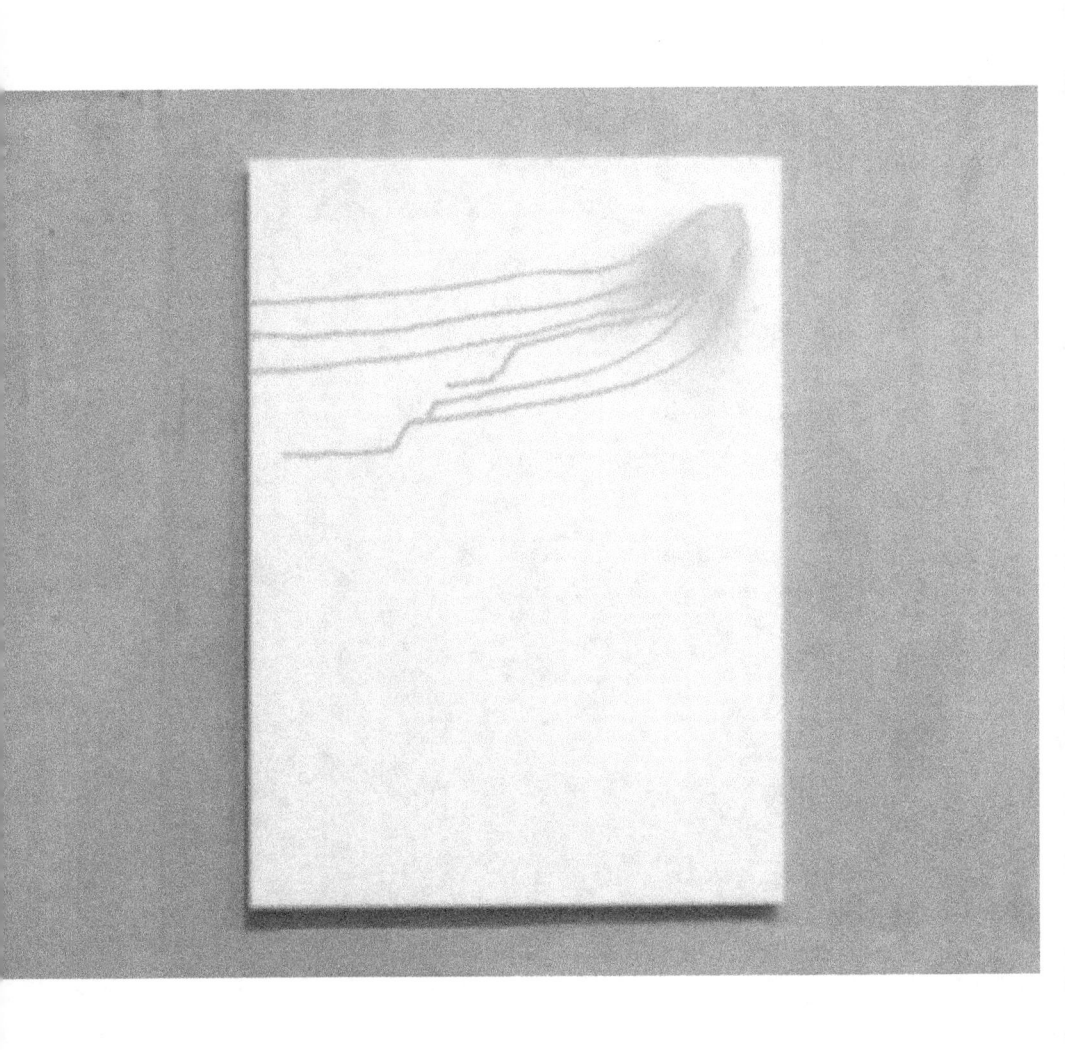

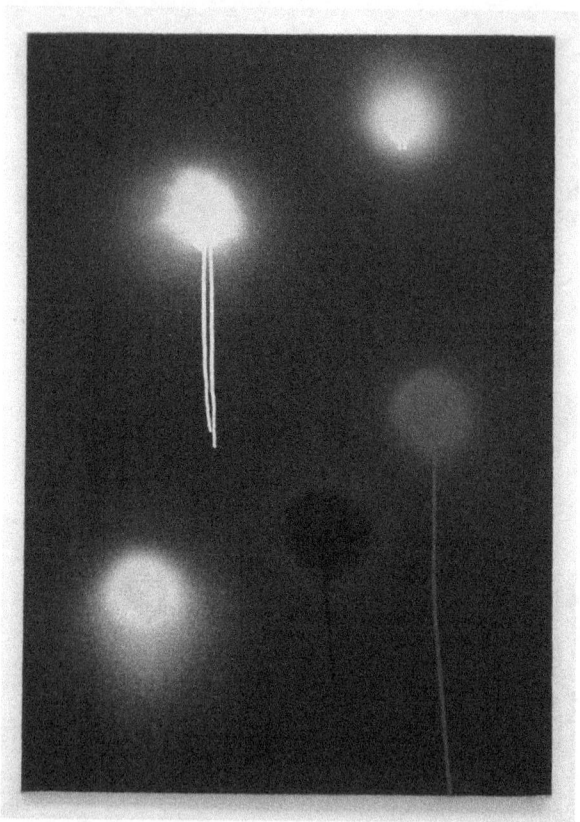

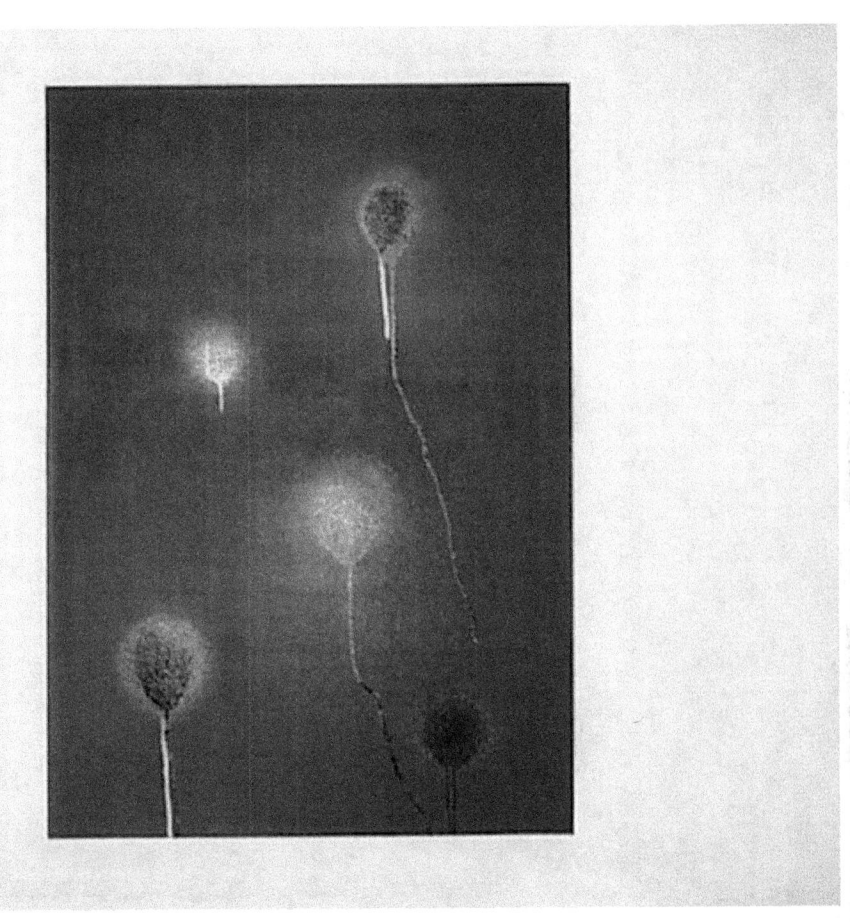

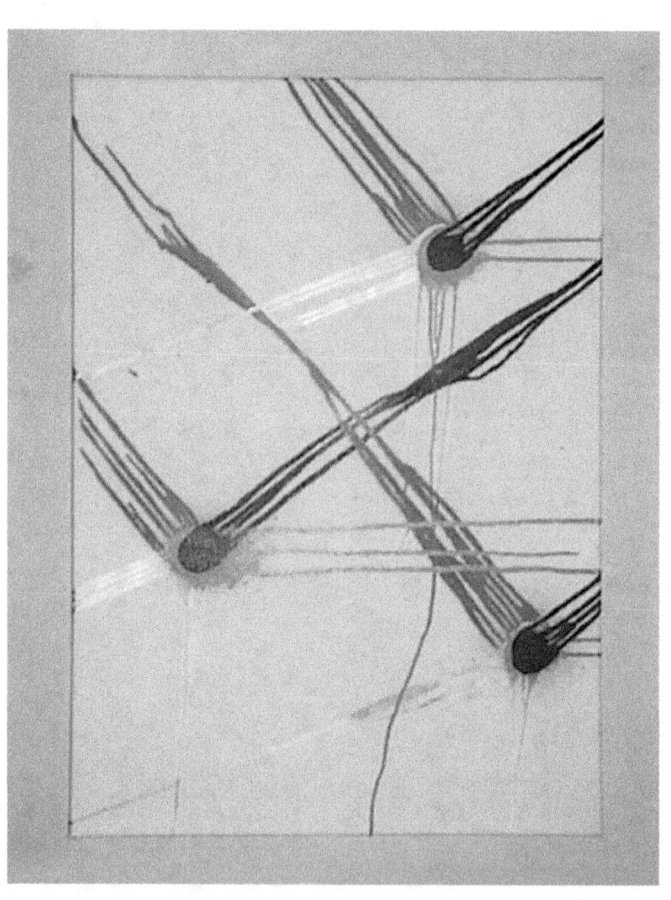

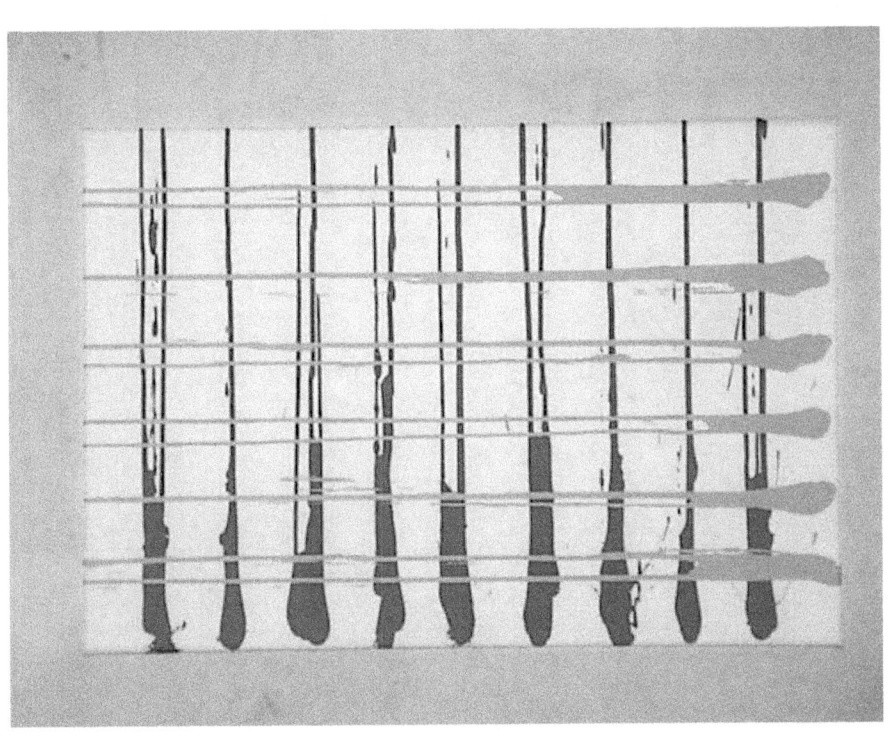

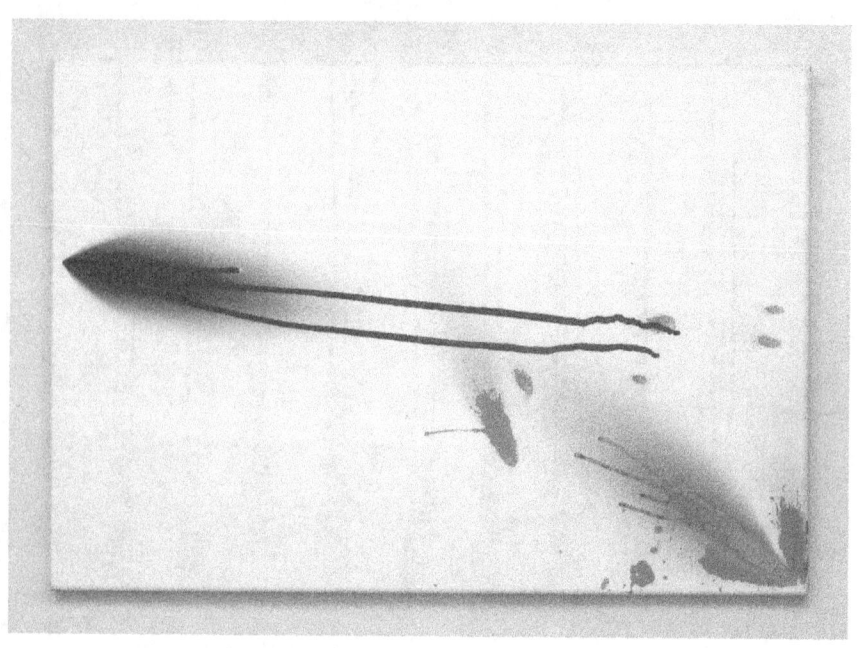

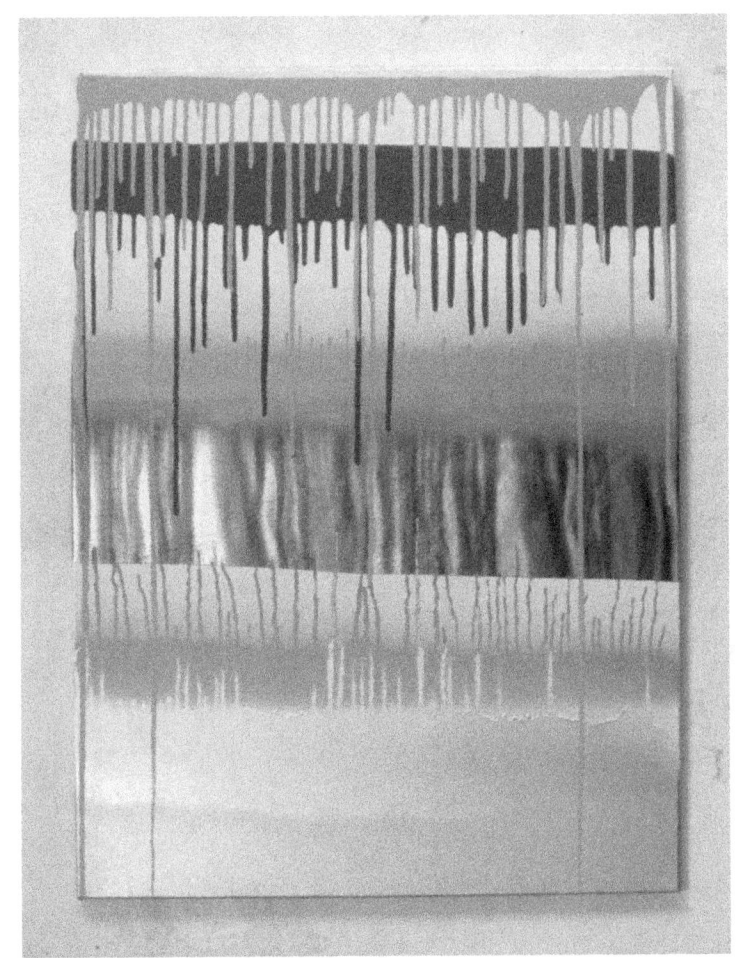

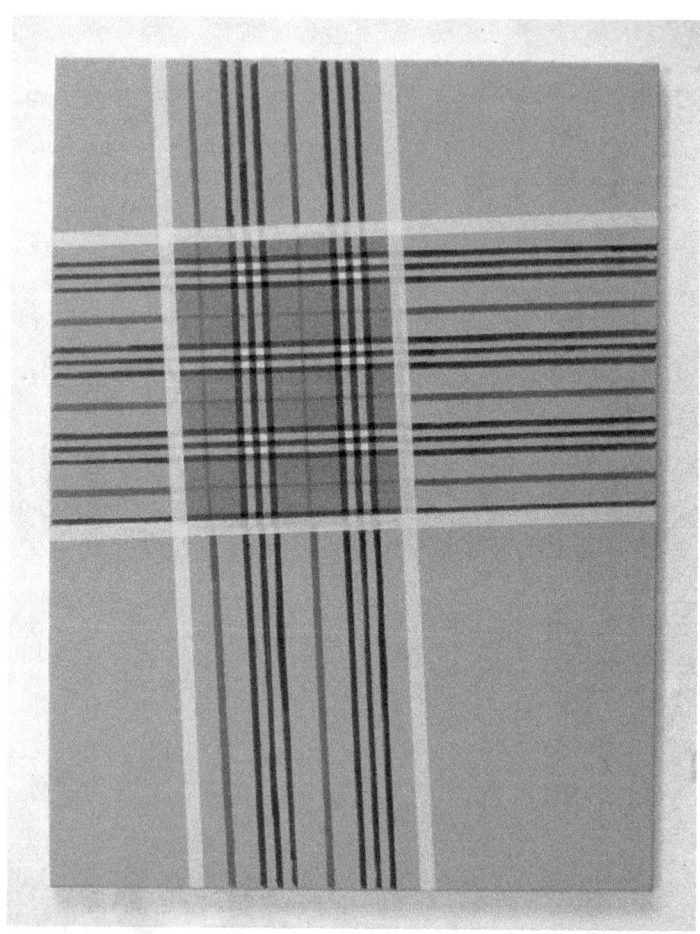

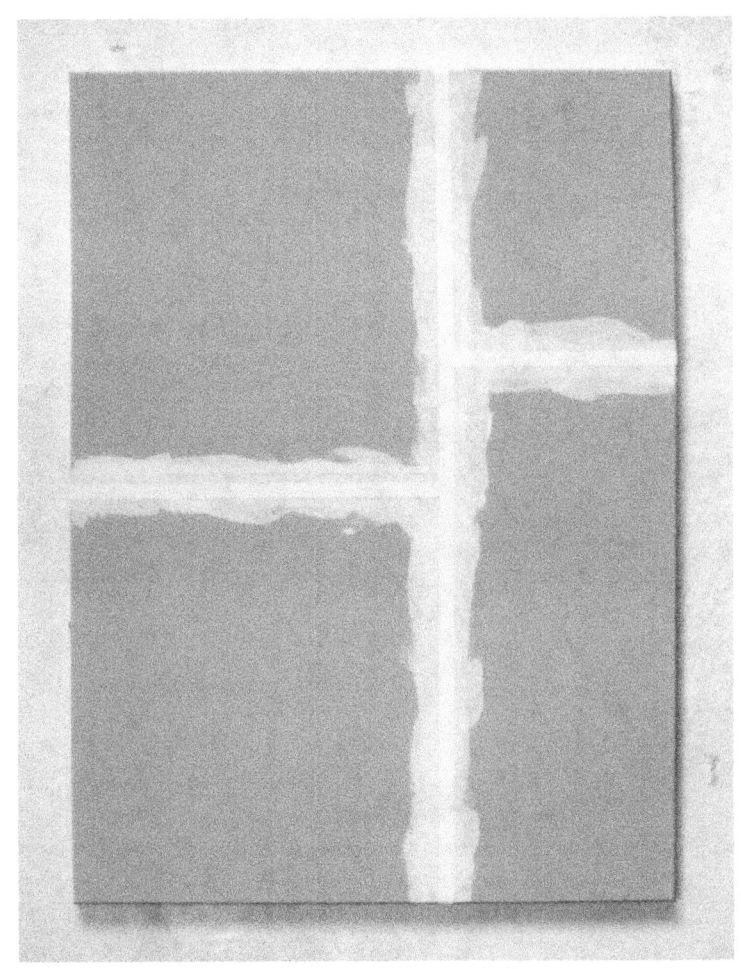

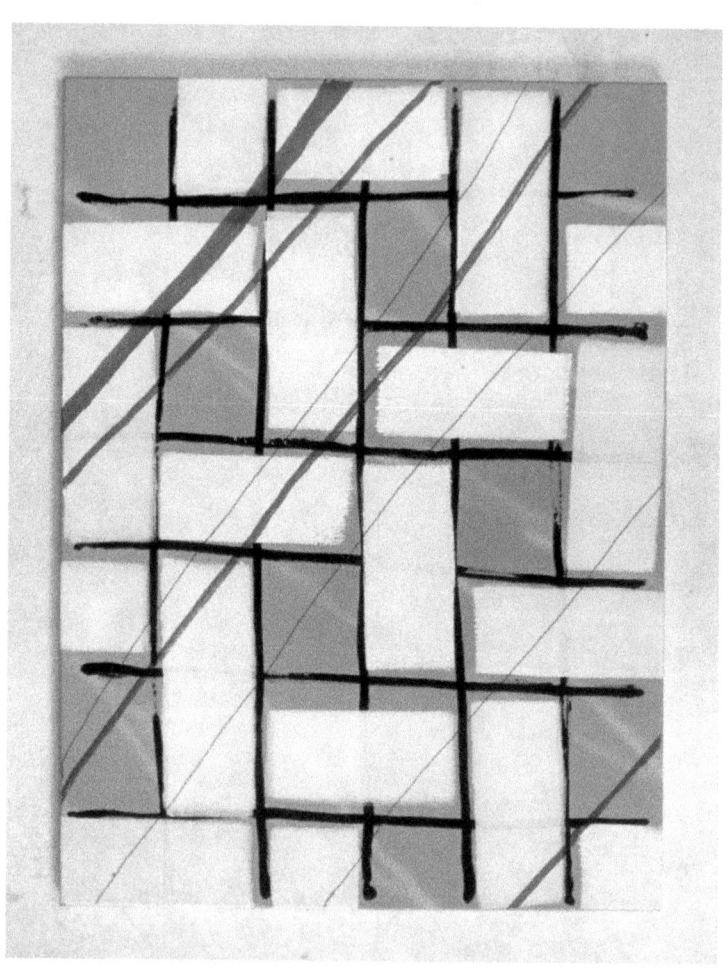

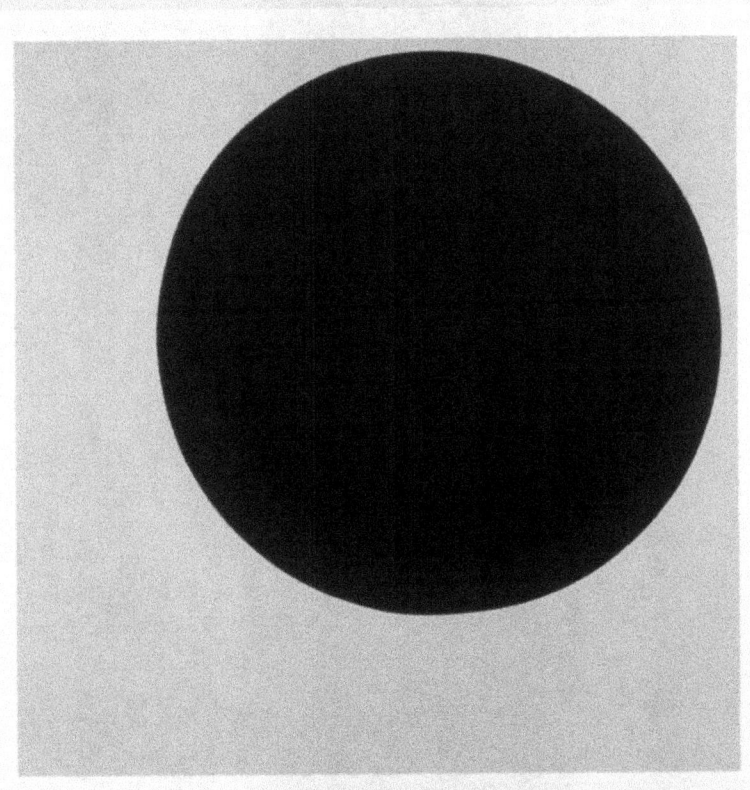

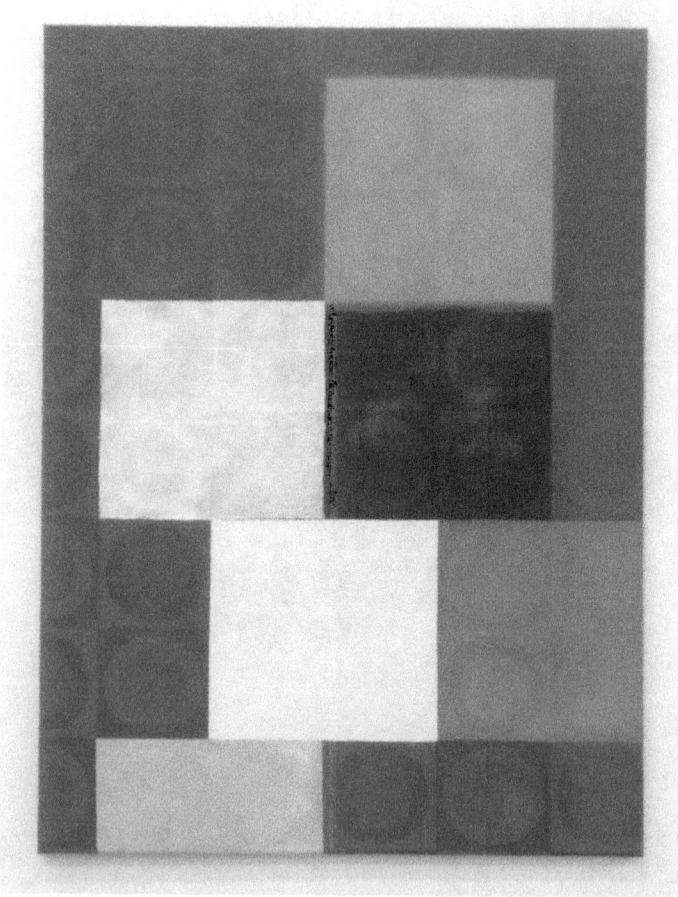

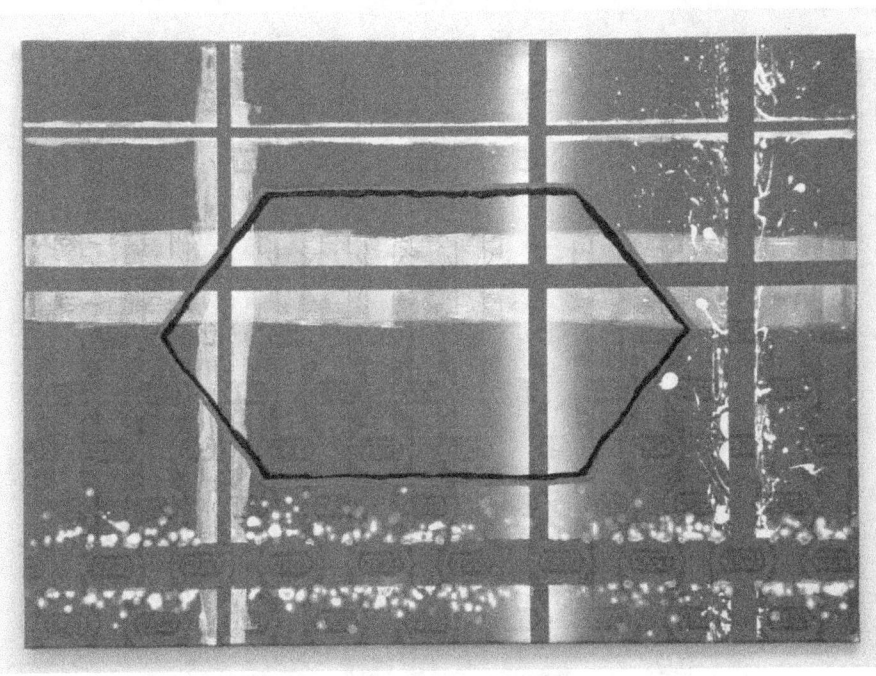

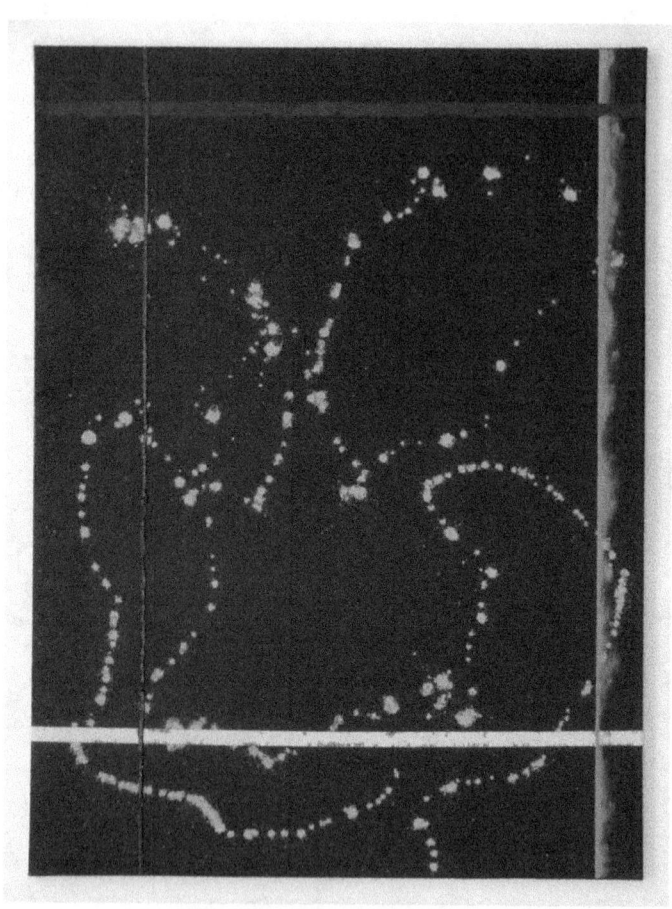

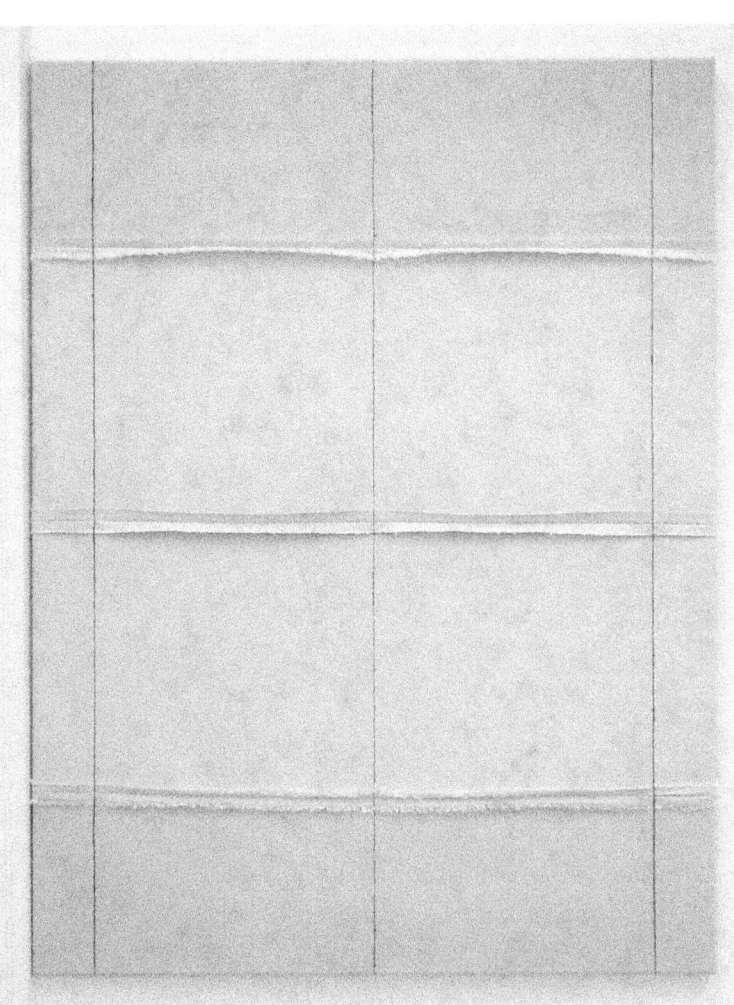

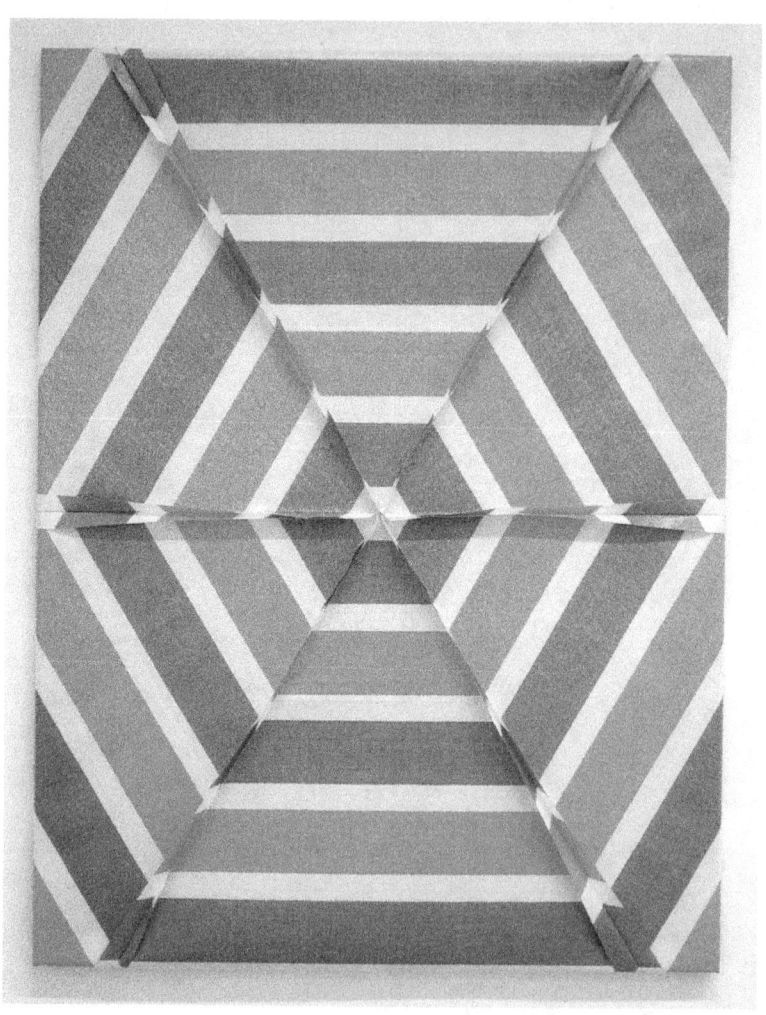

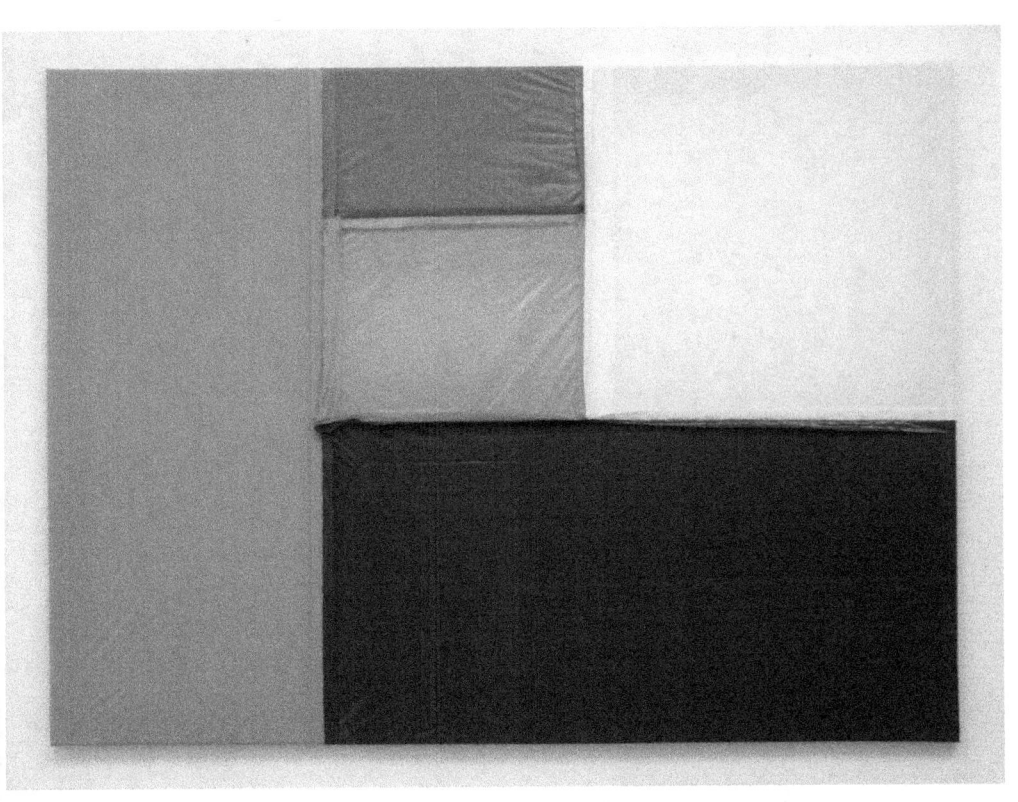

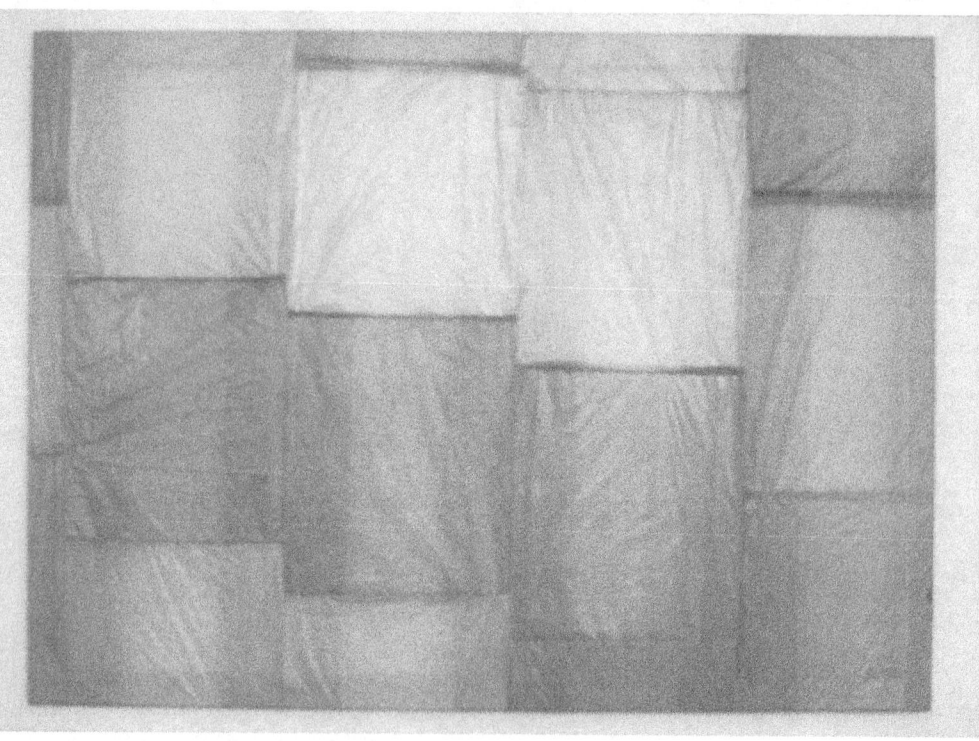

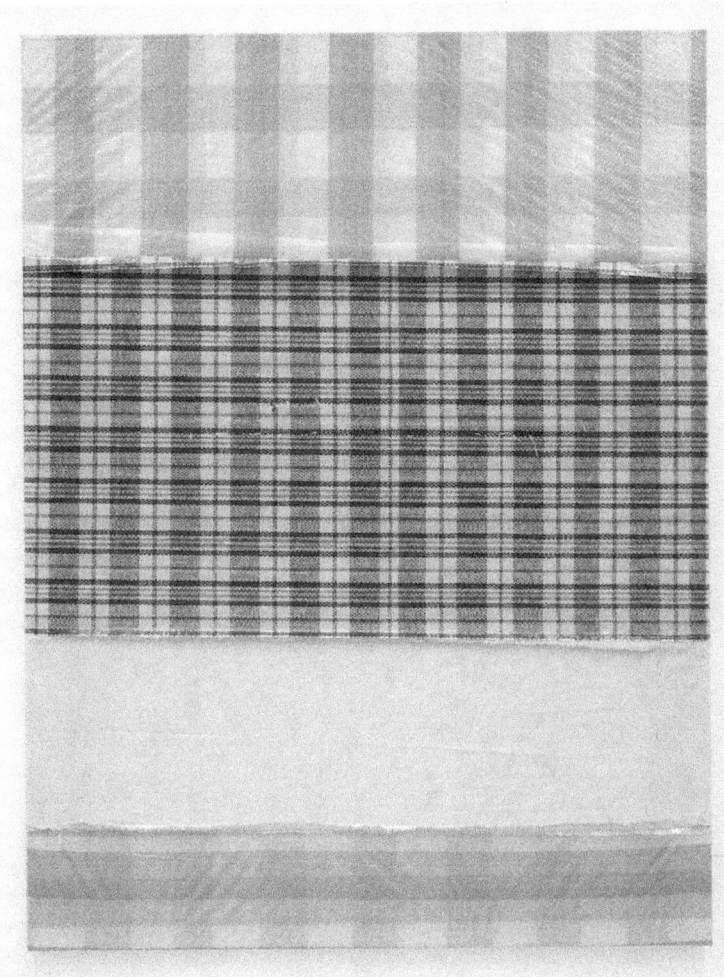

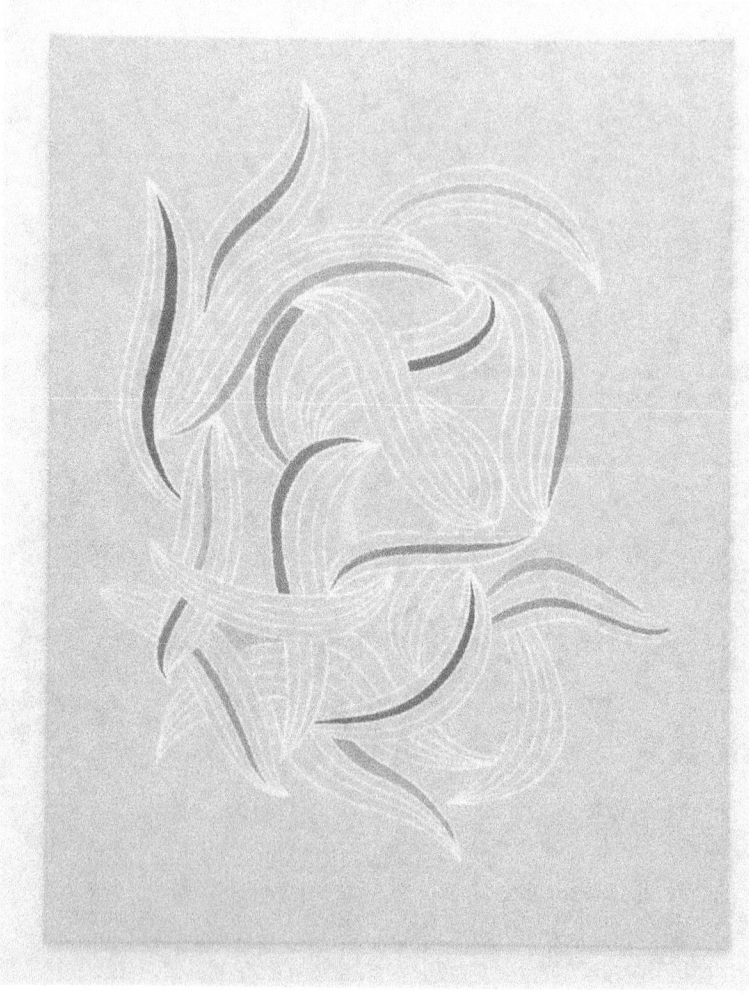

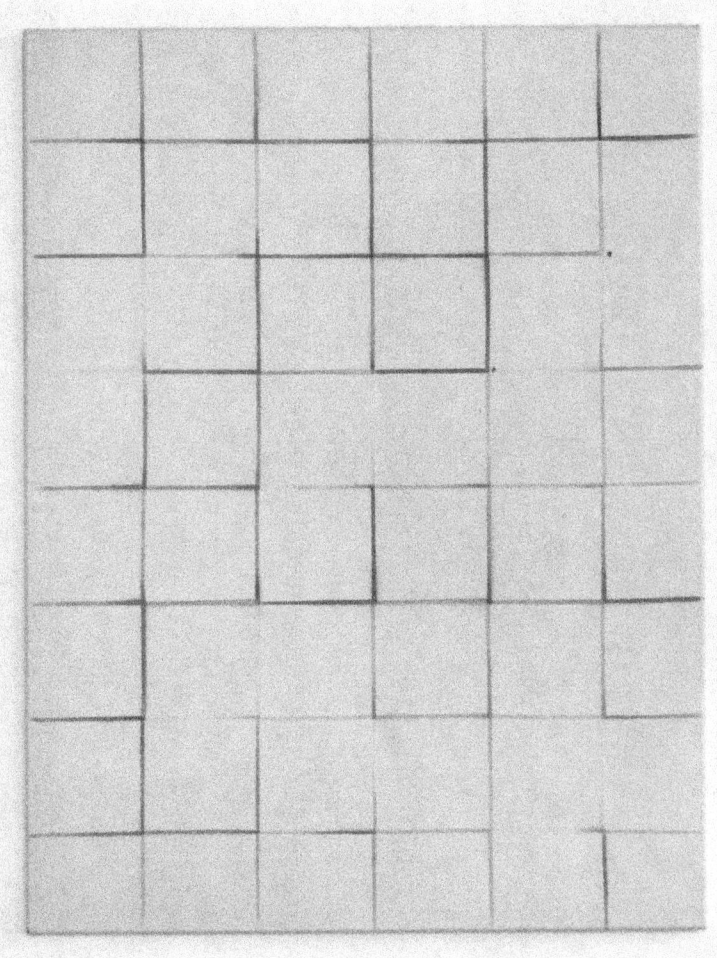

29

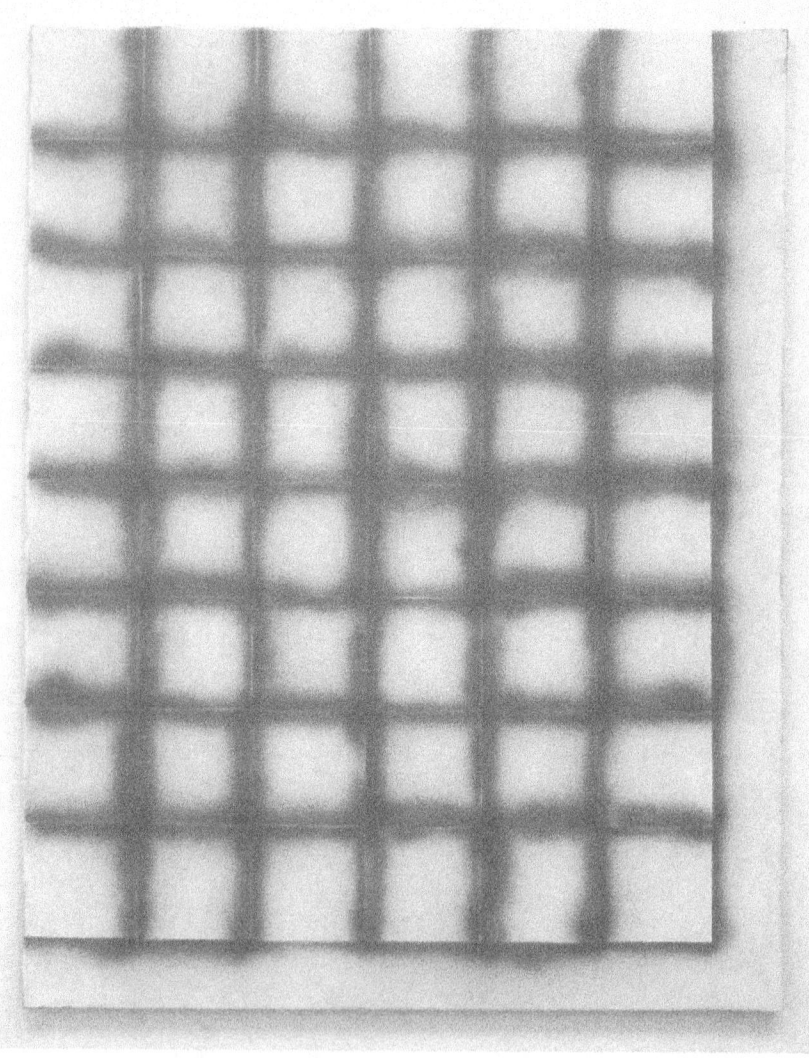

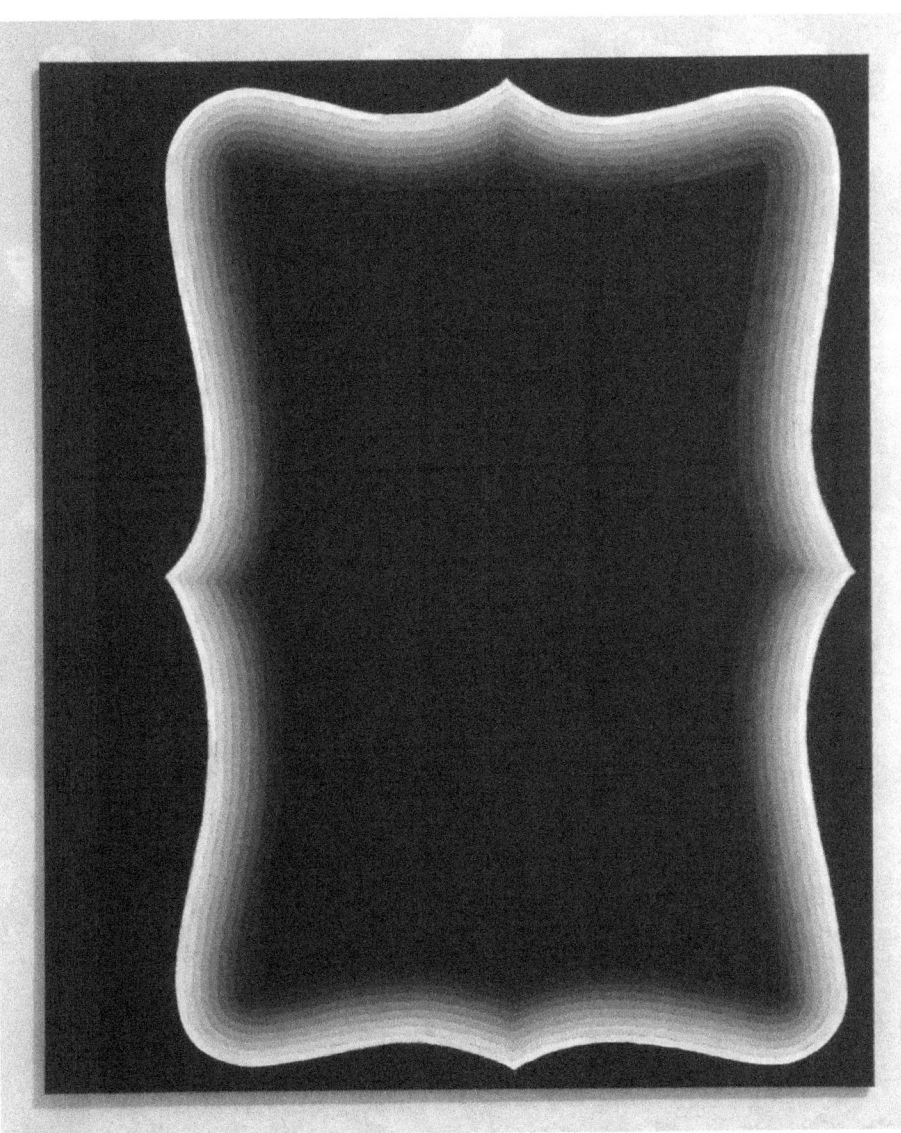

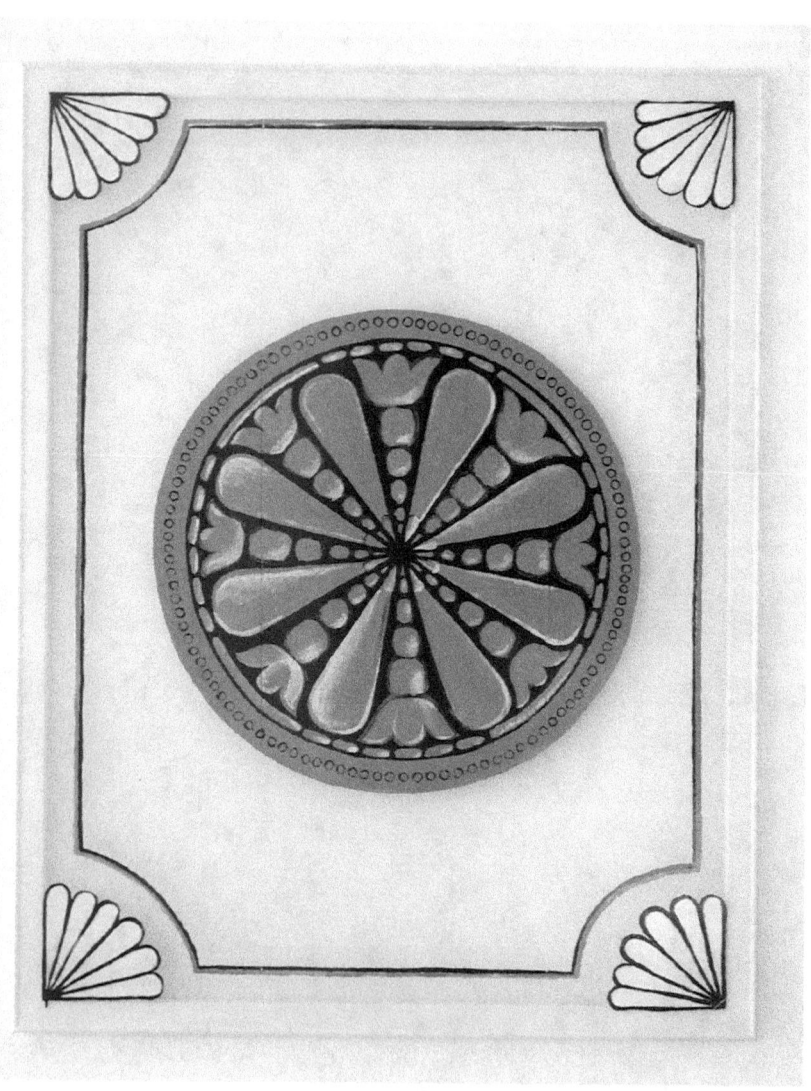

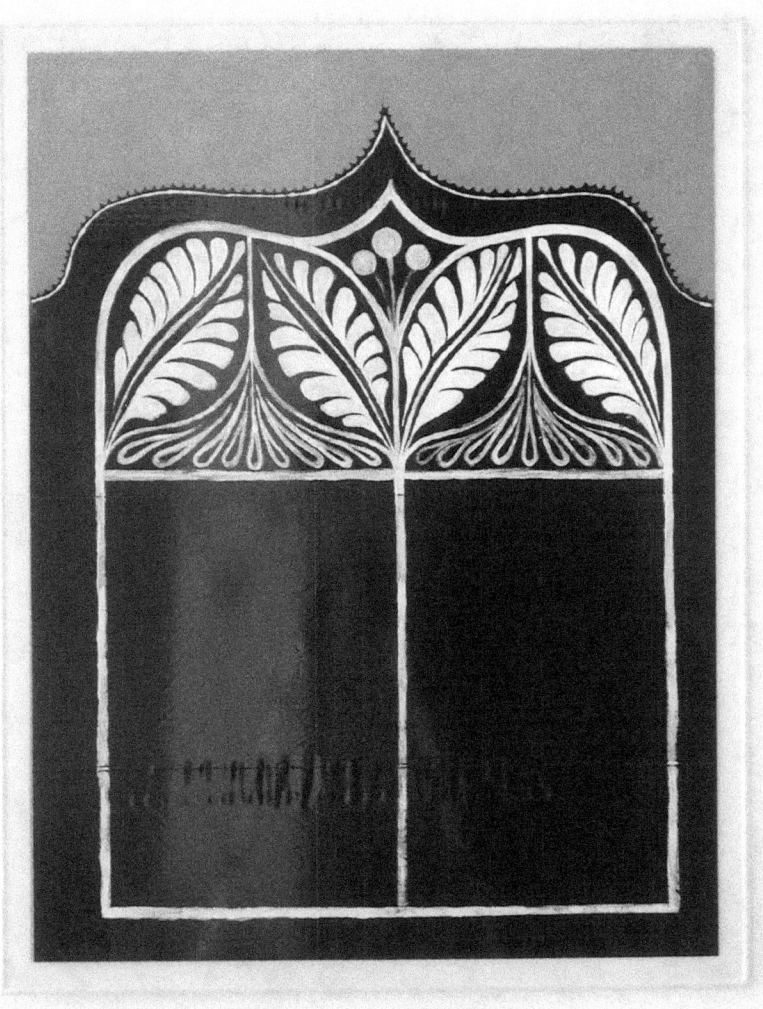

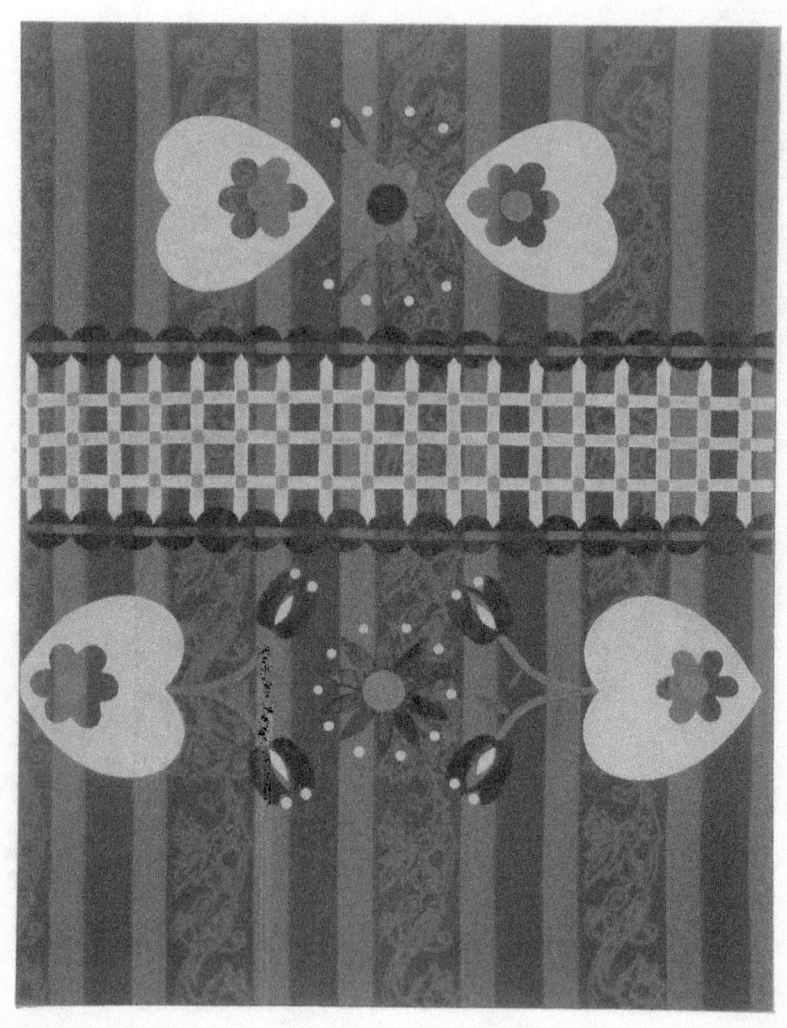

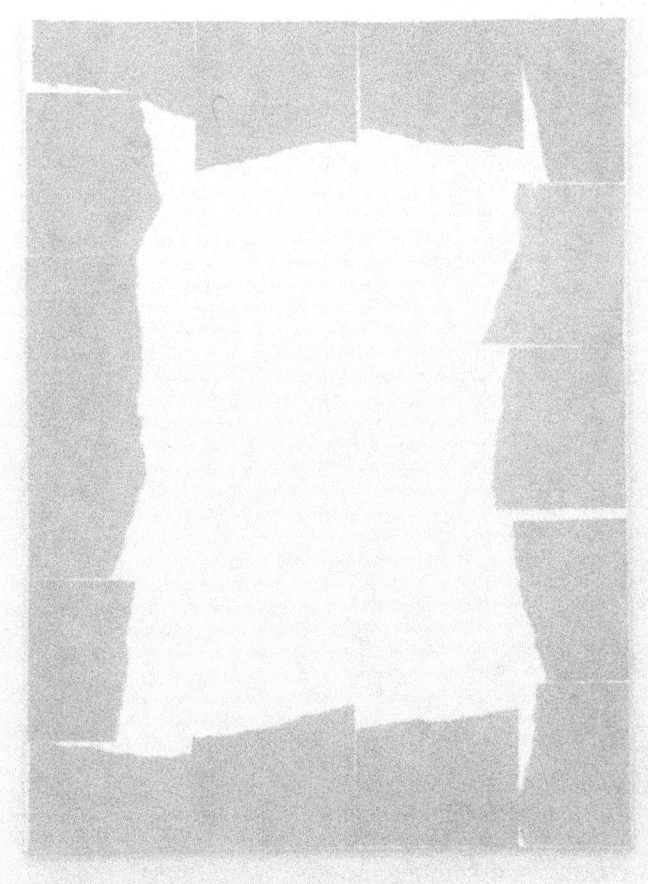

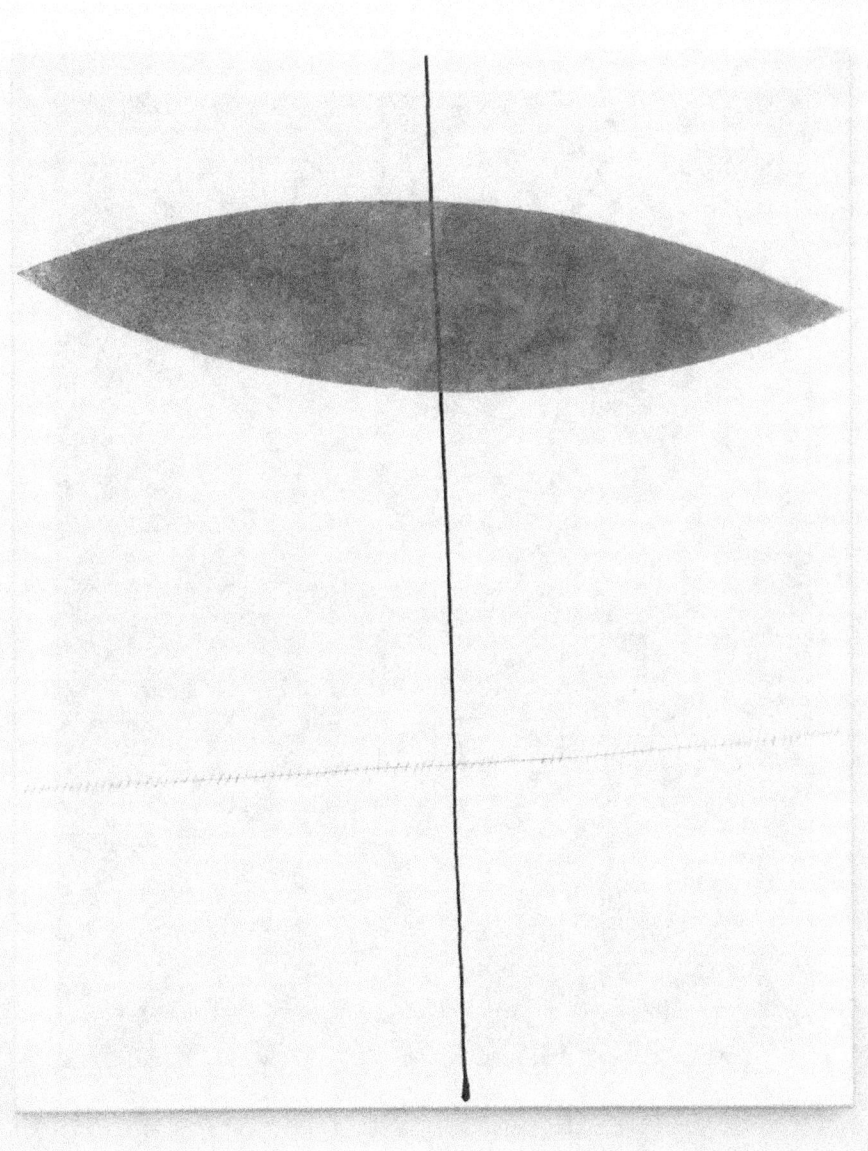

37

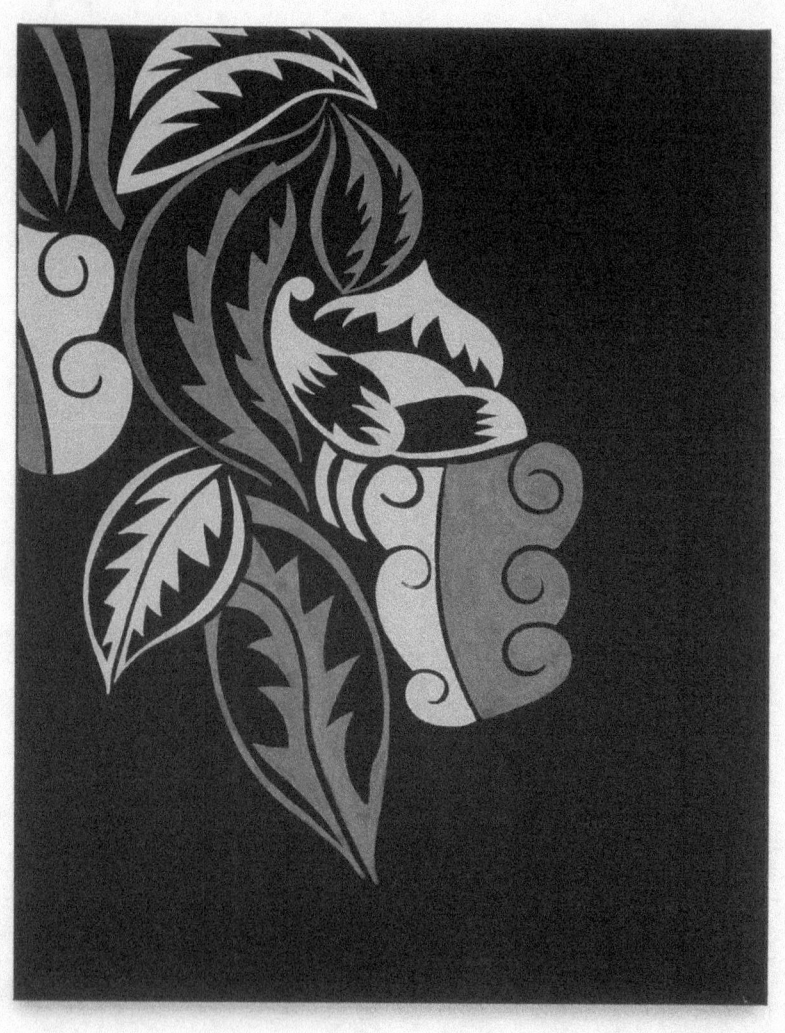

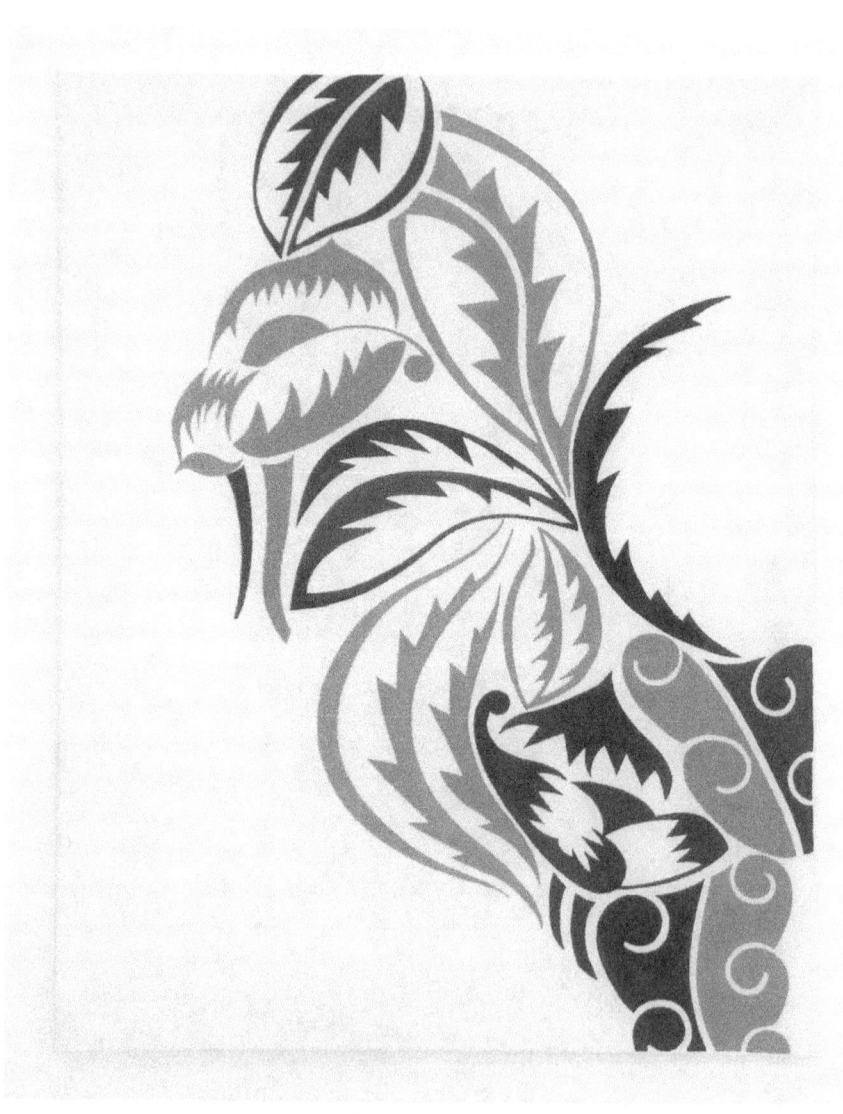

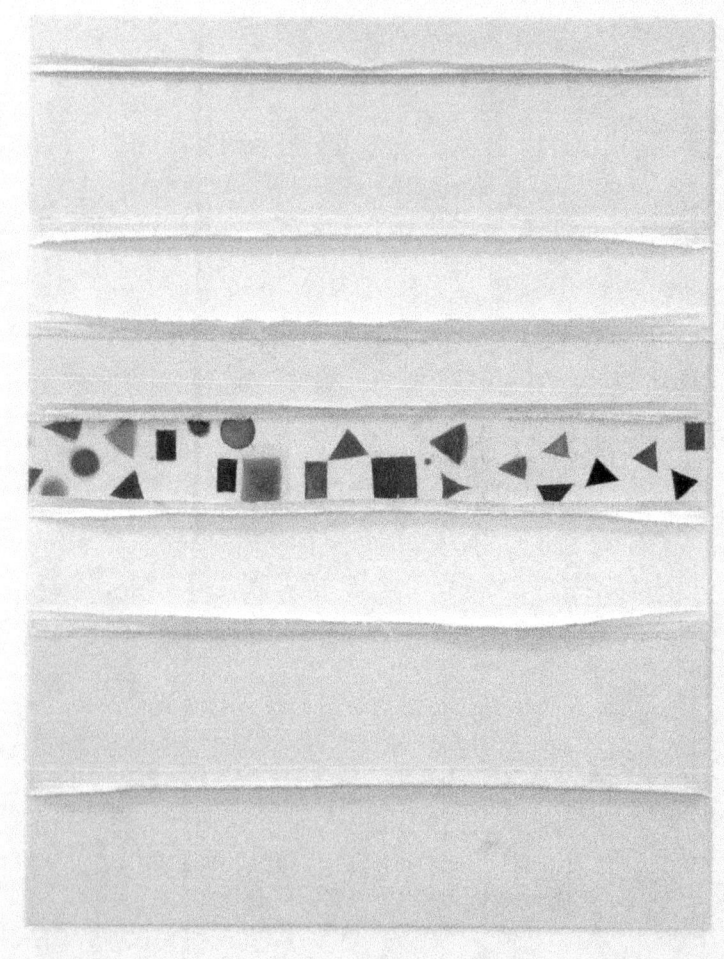

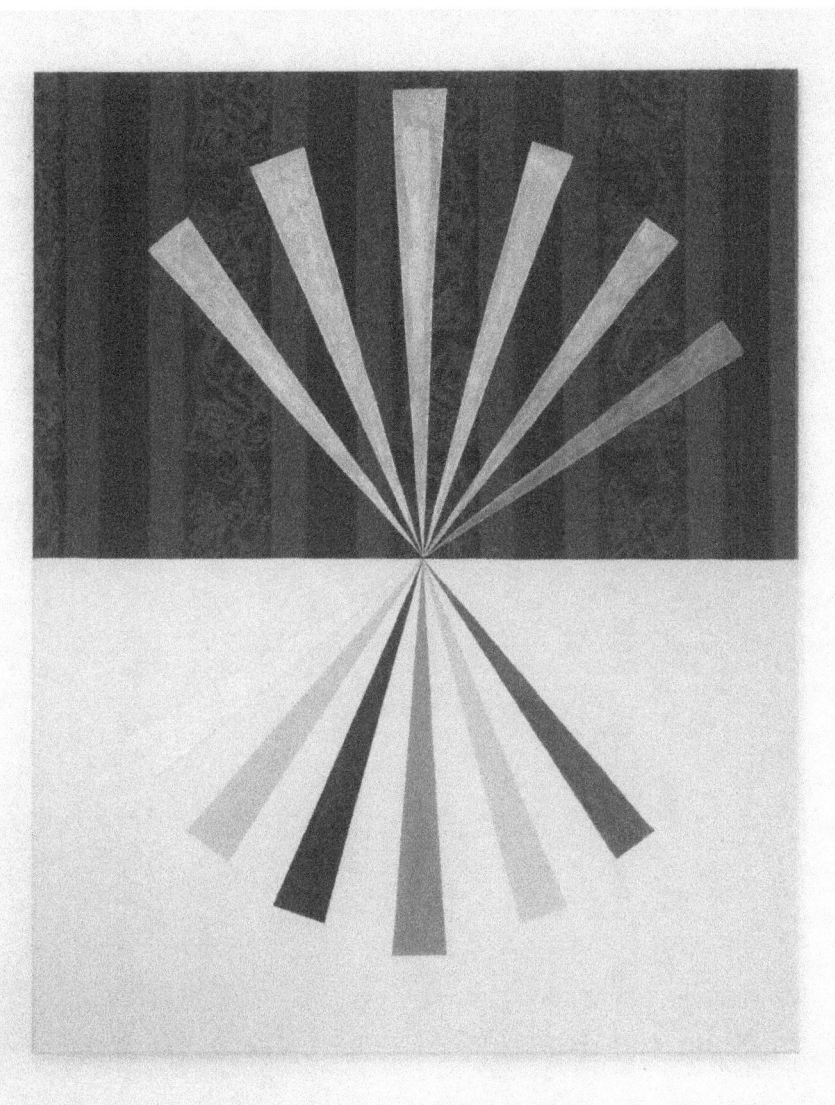

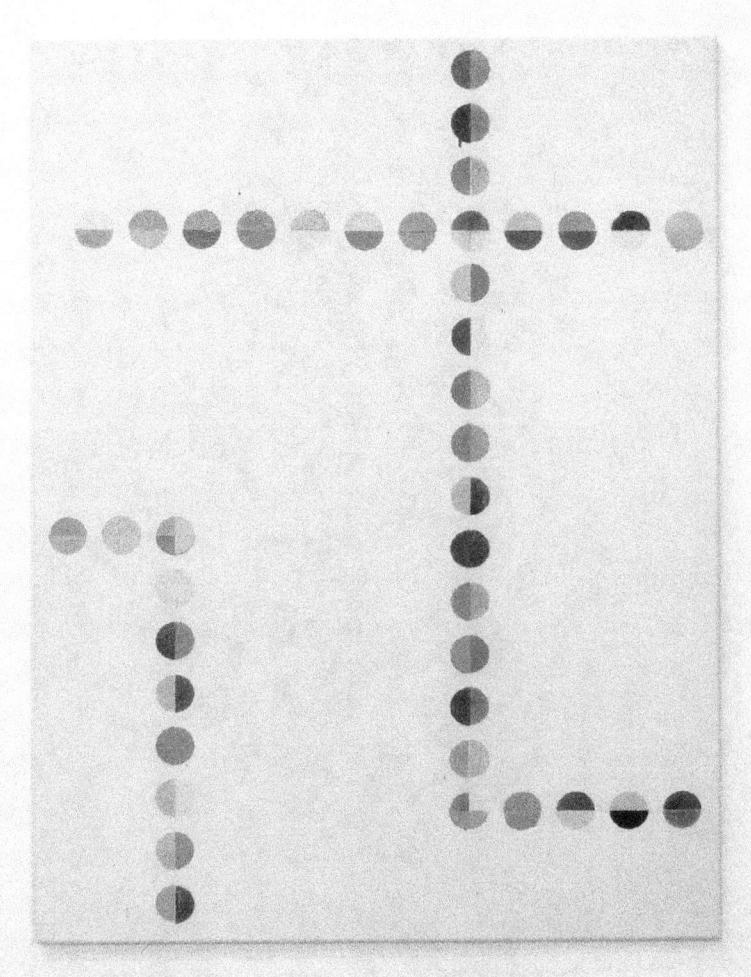

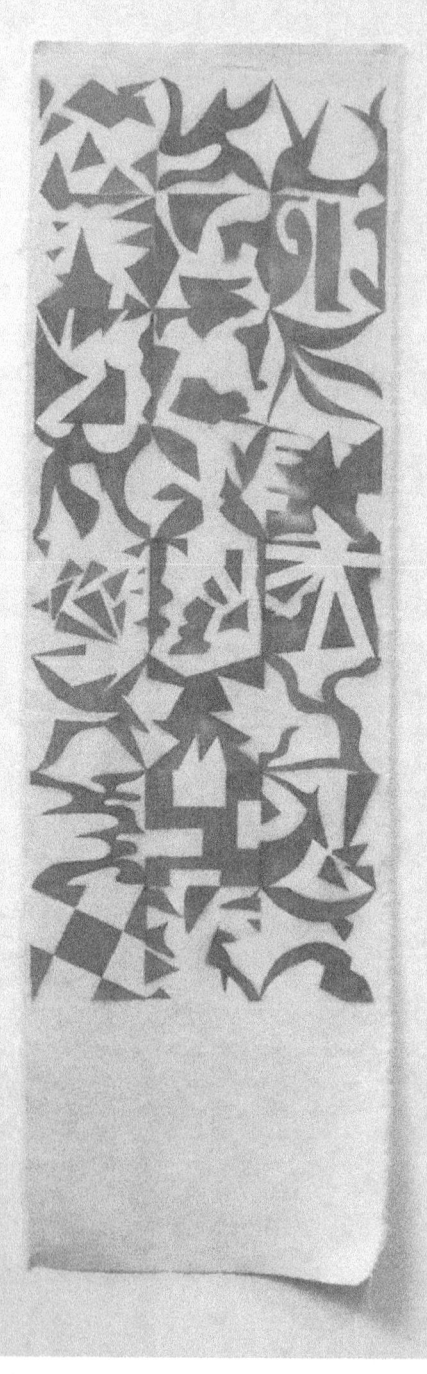

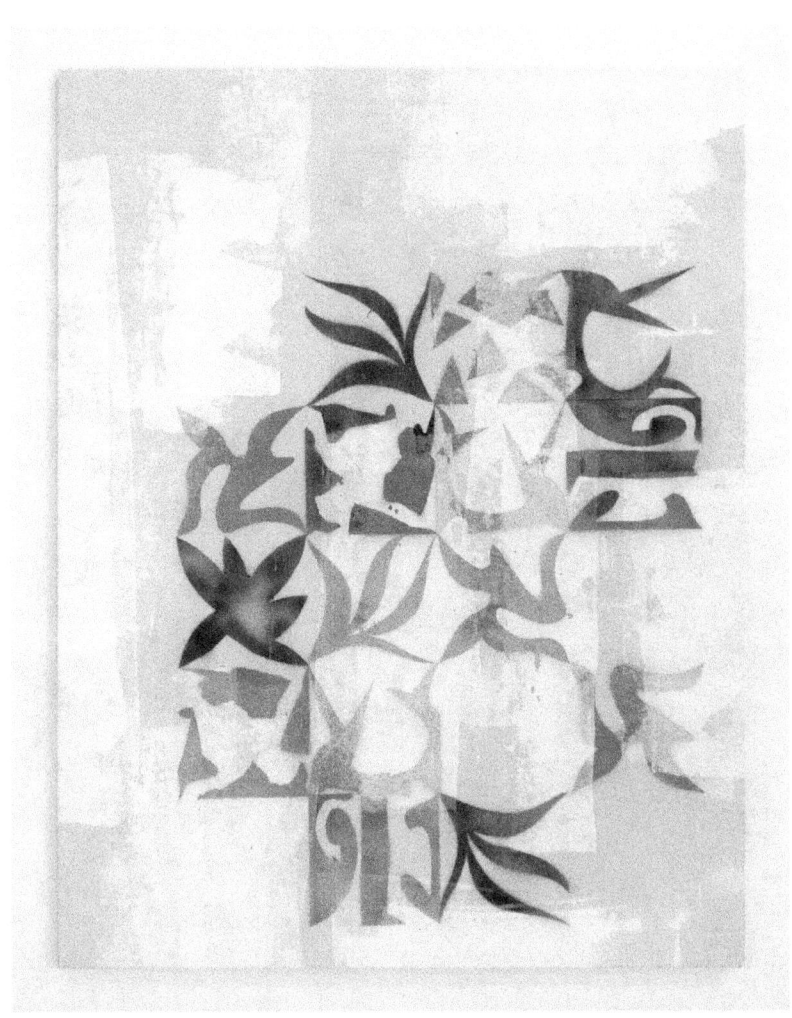

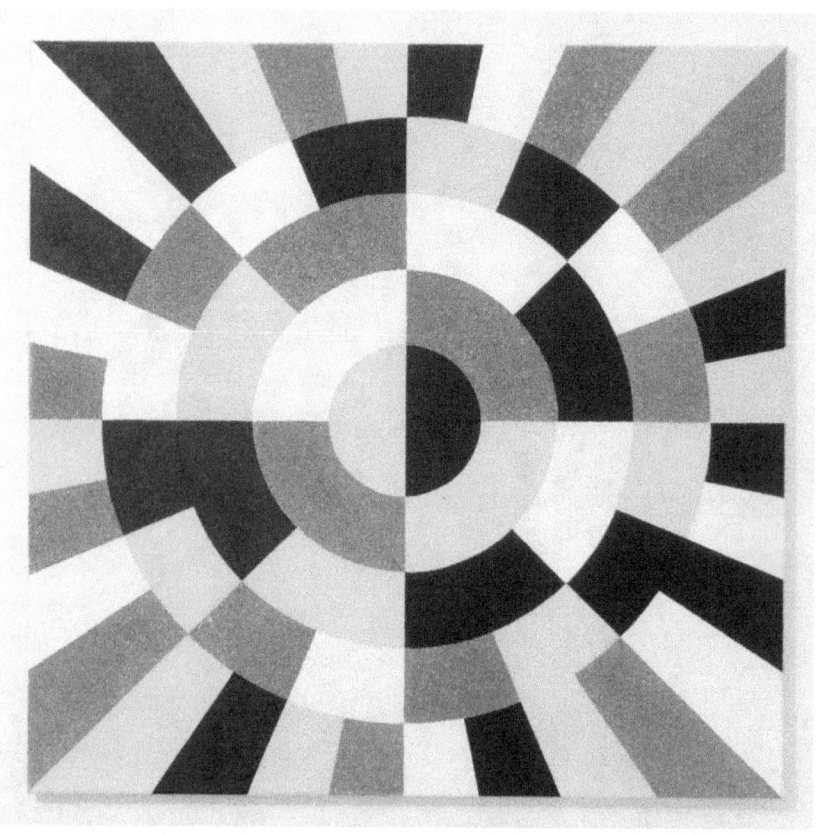

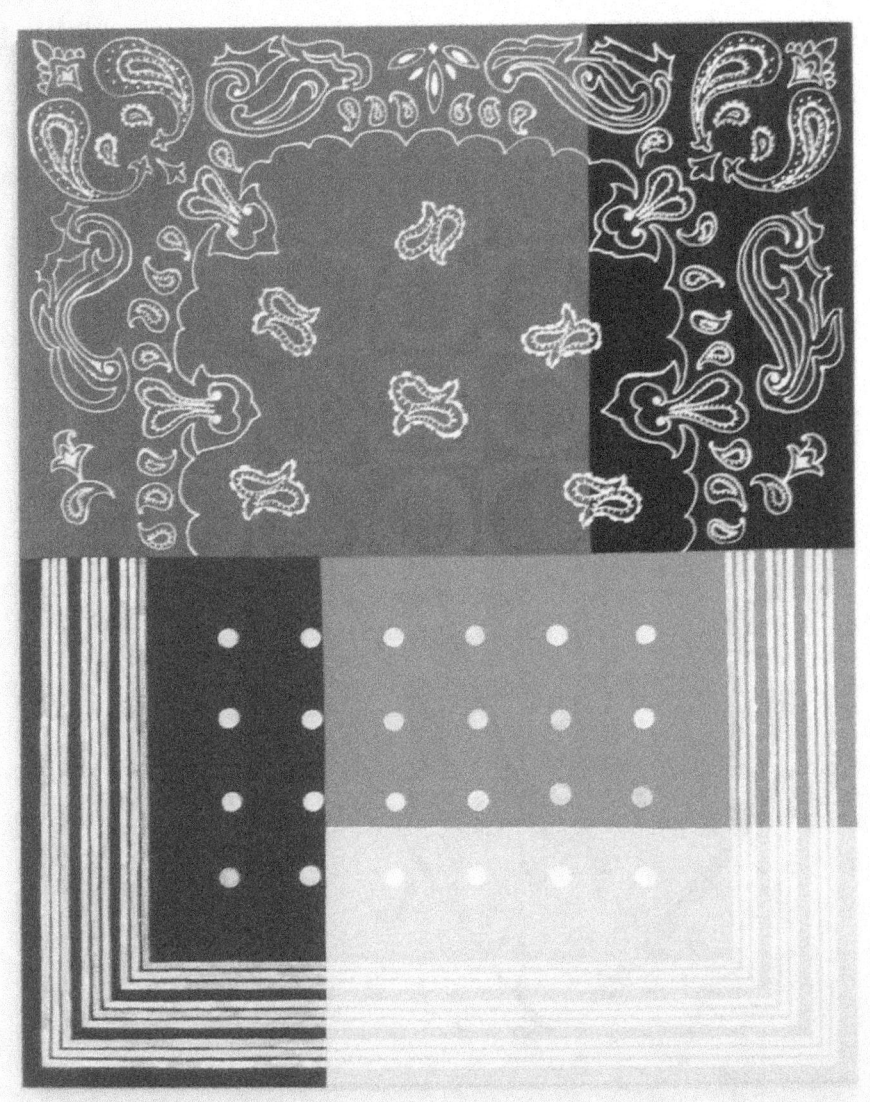

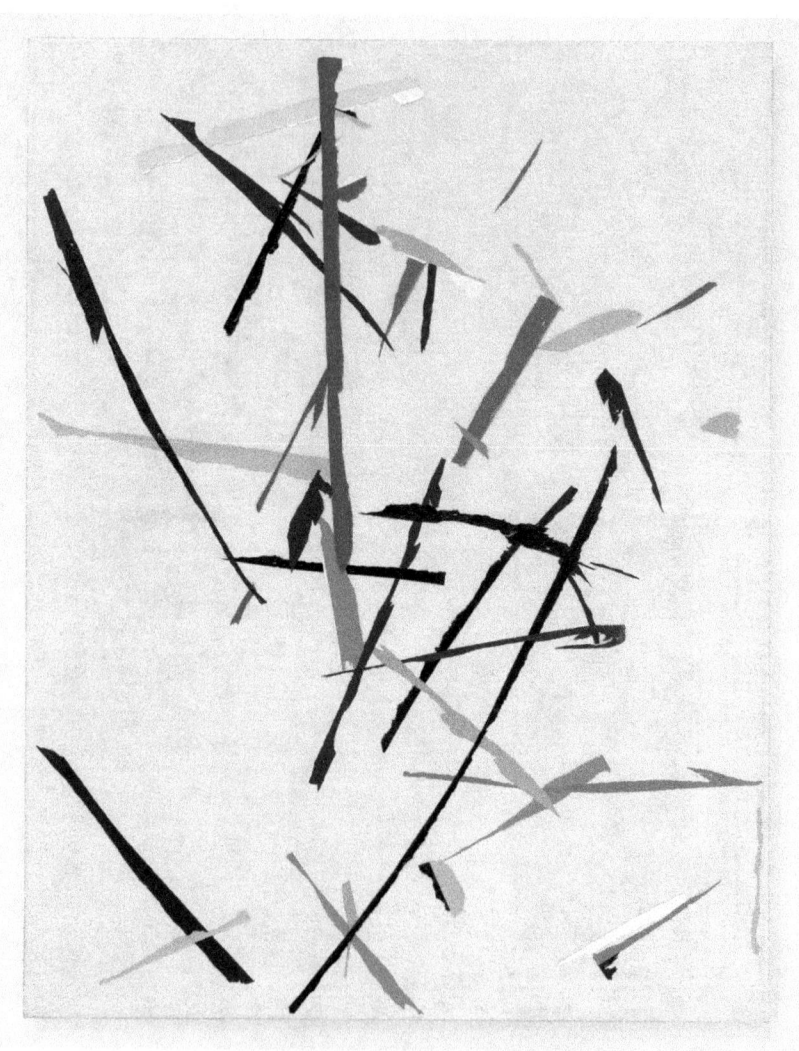

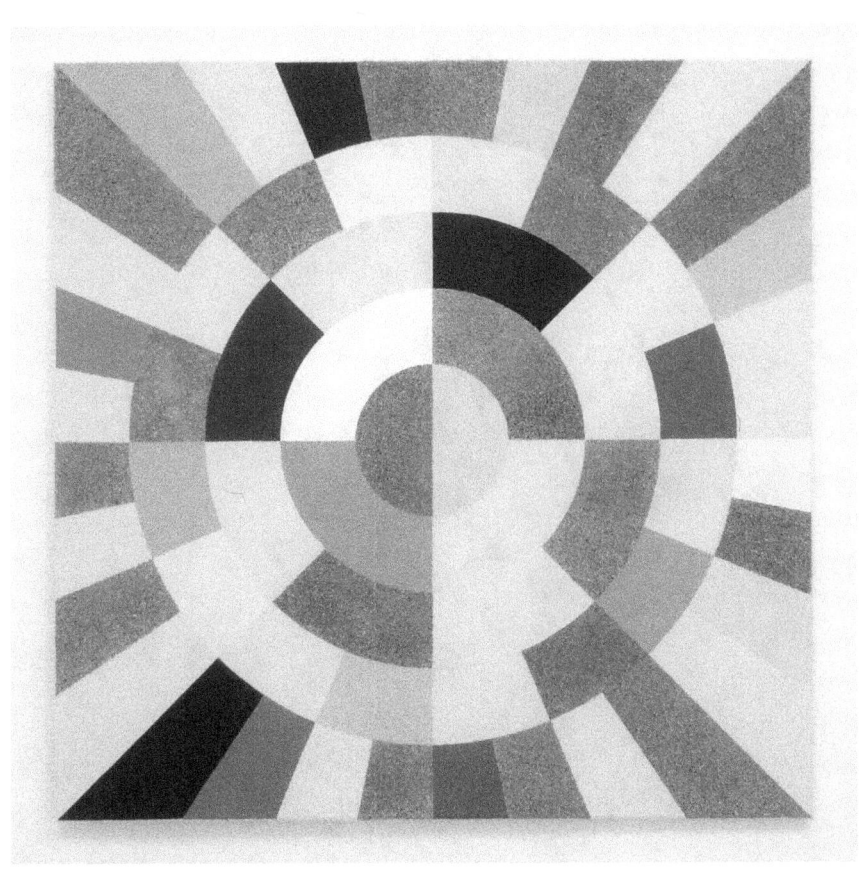

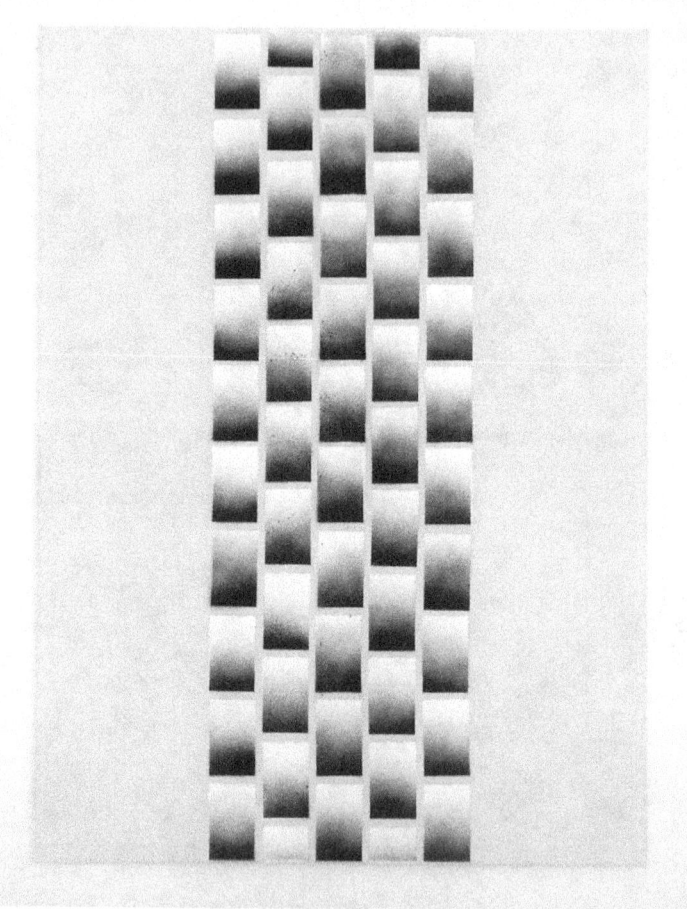

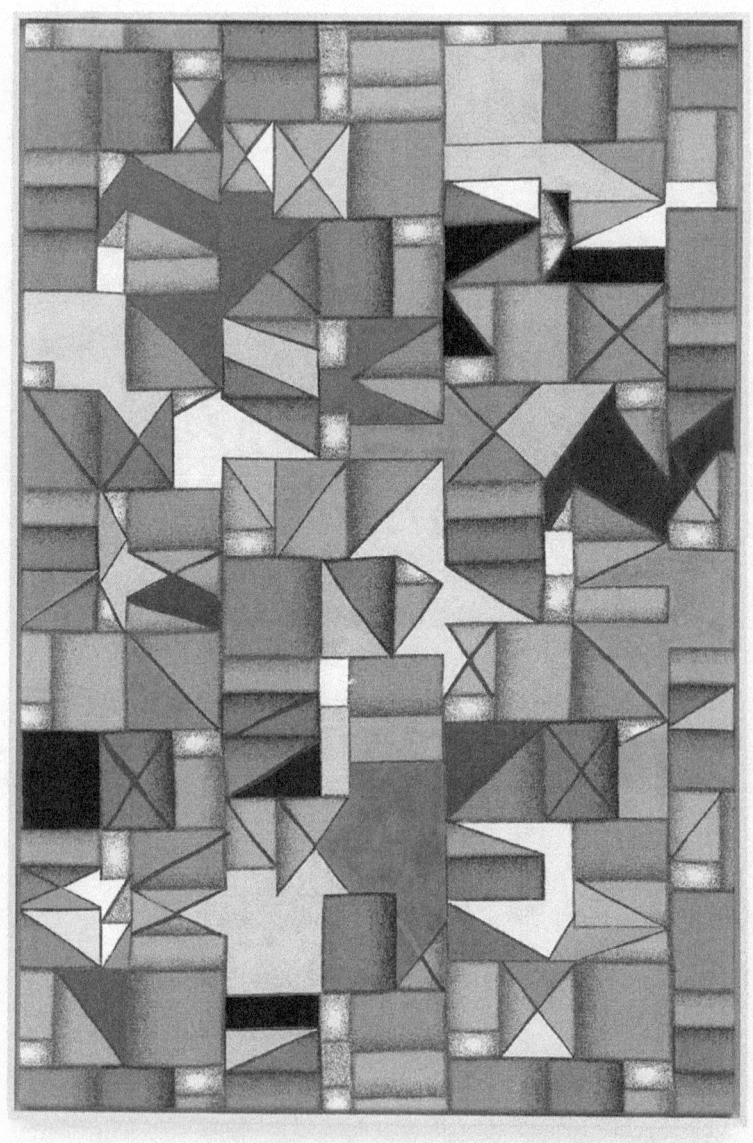

54

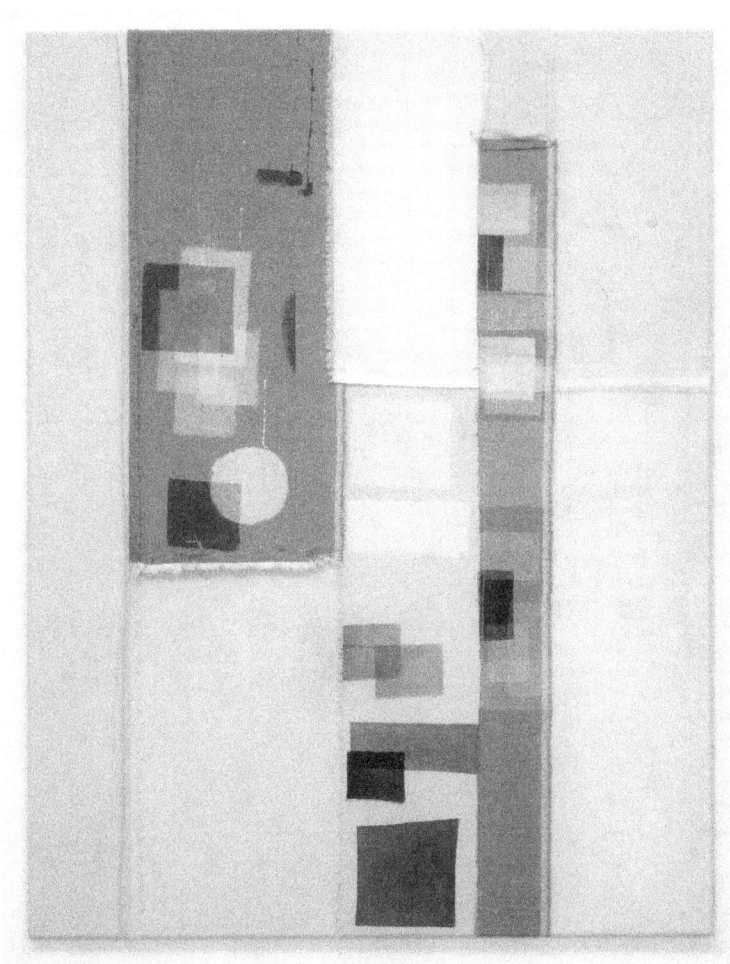

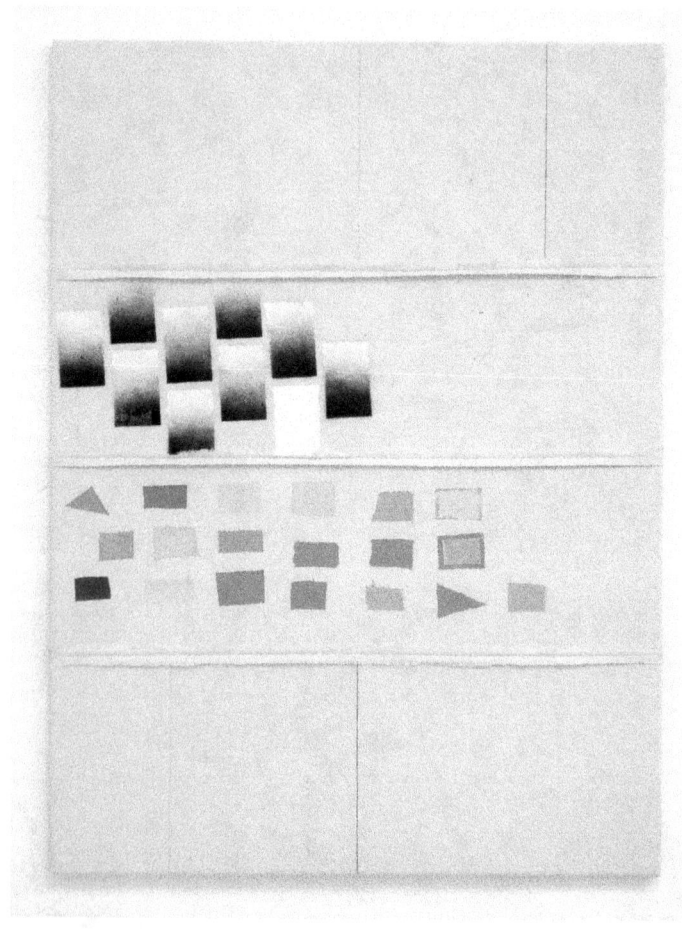

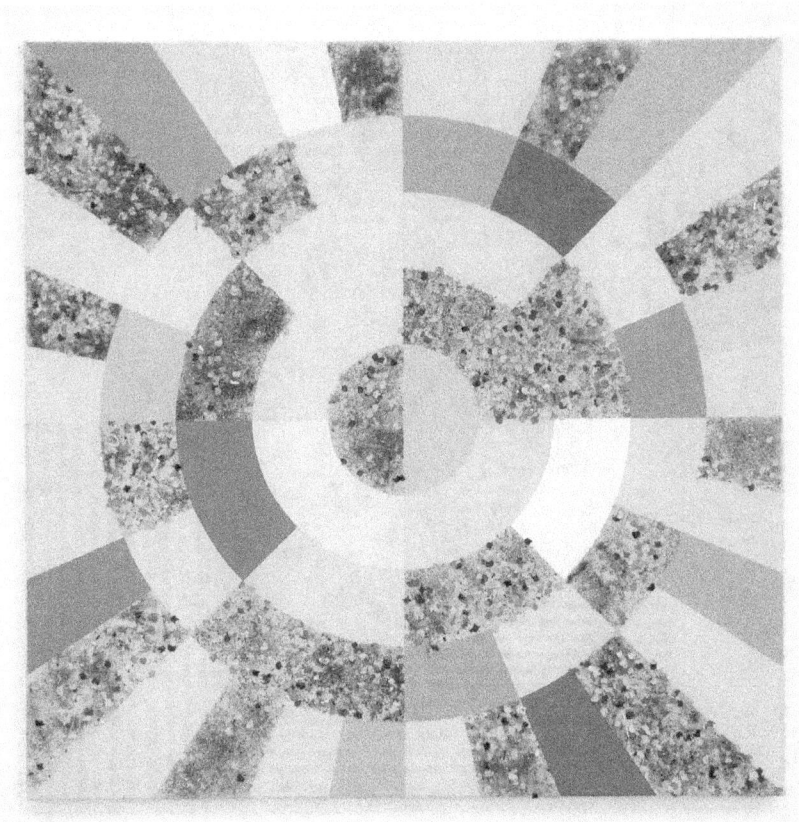

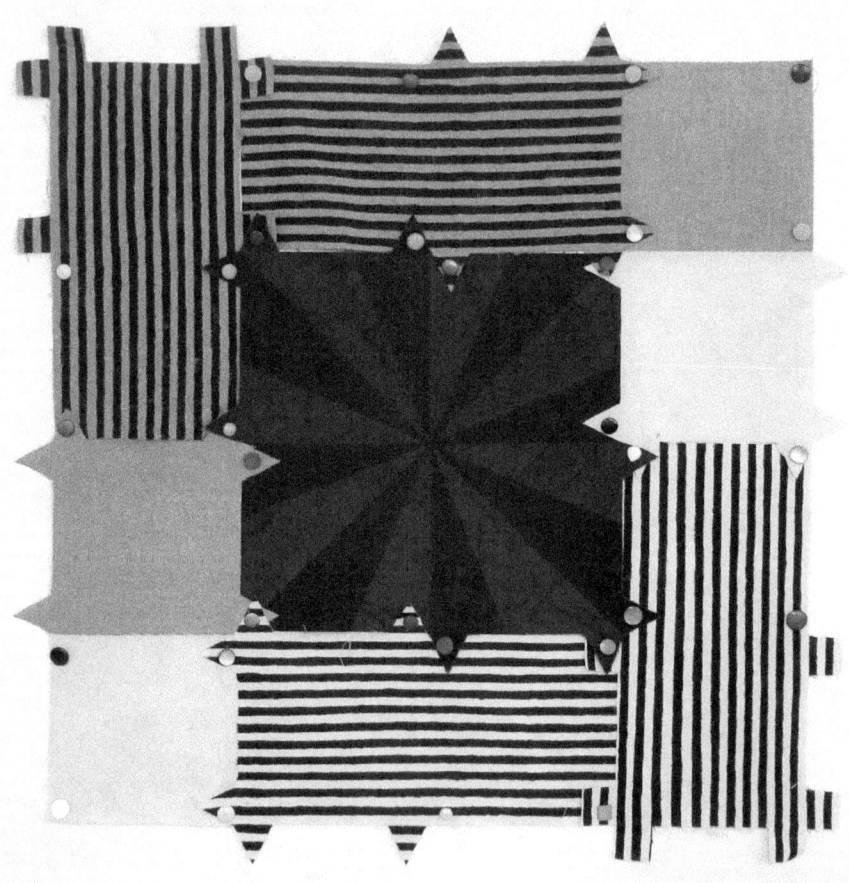

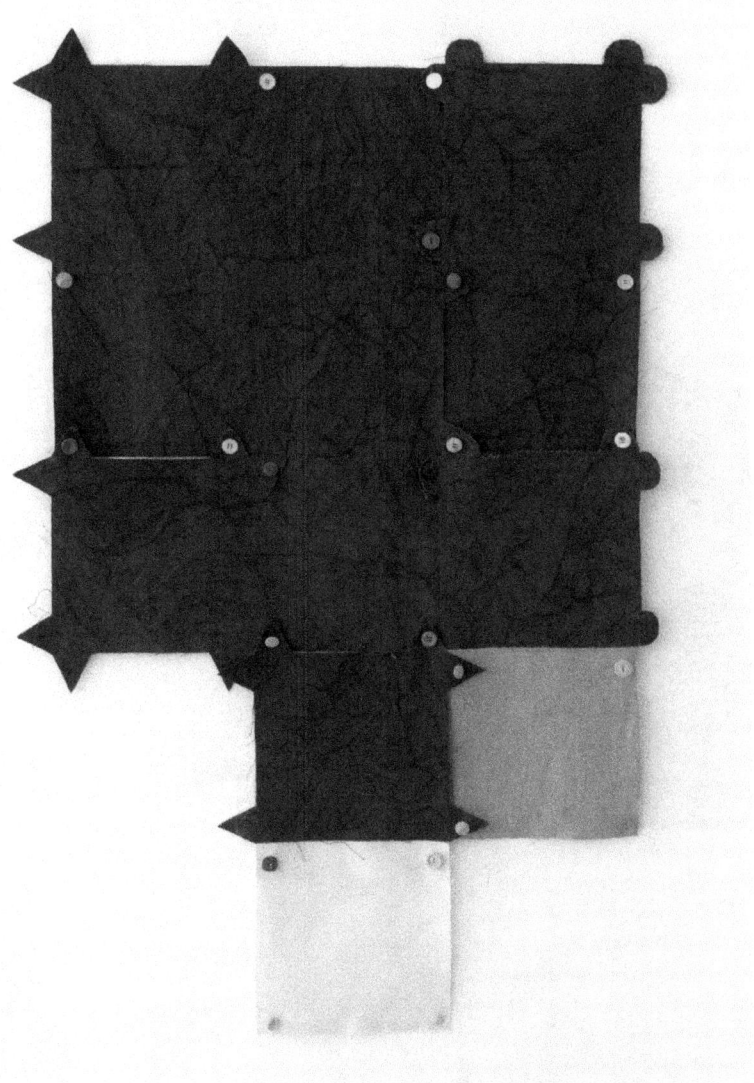

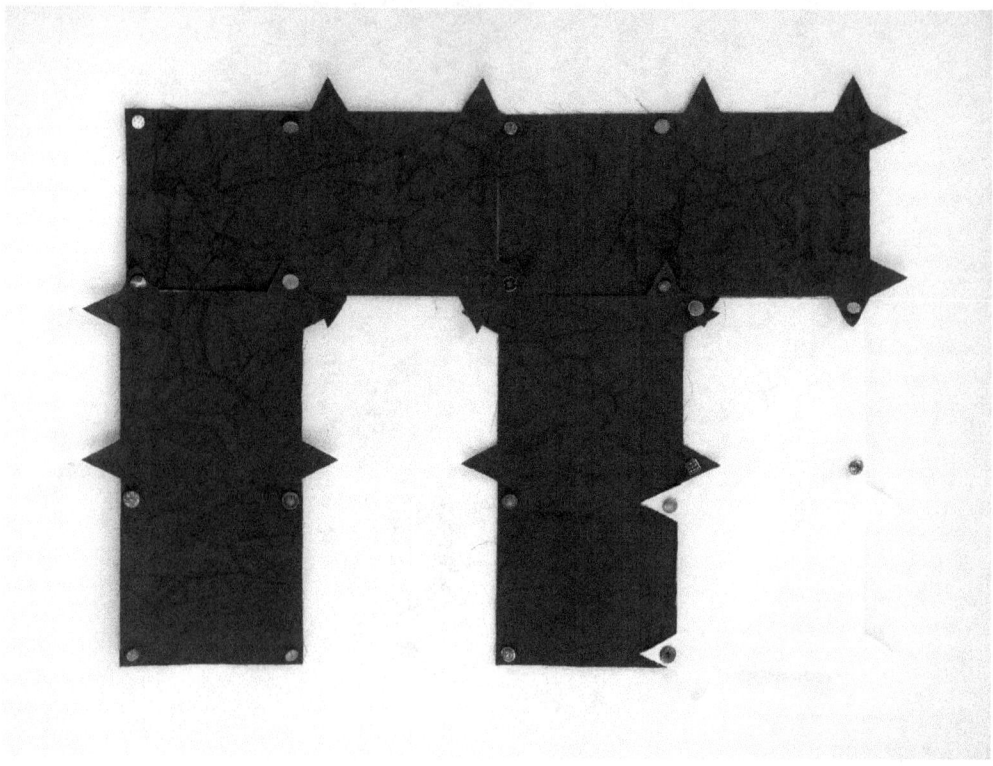

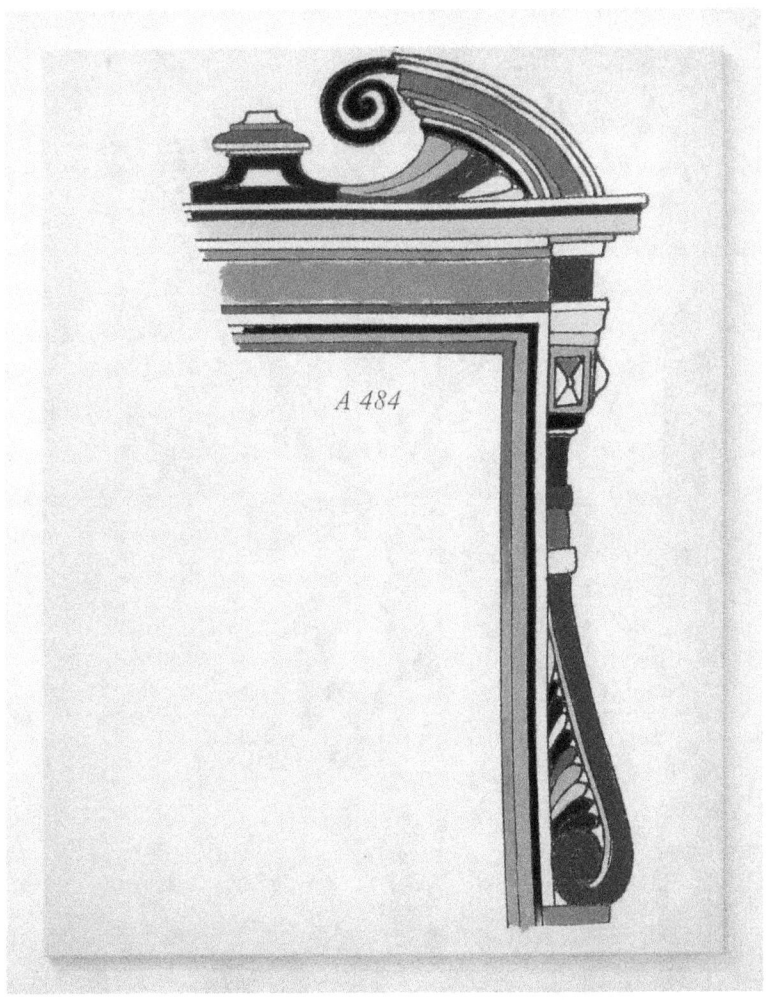

A 484

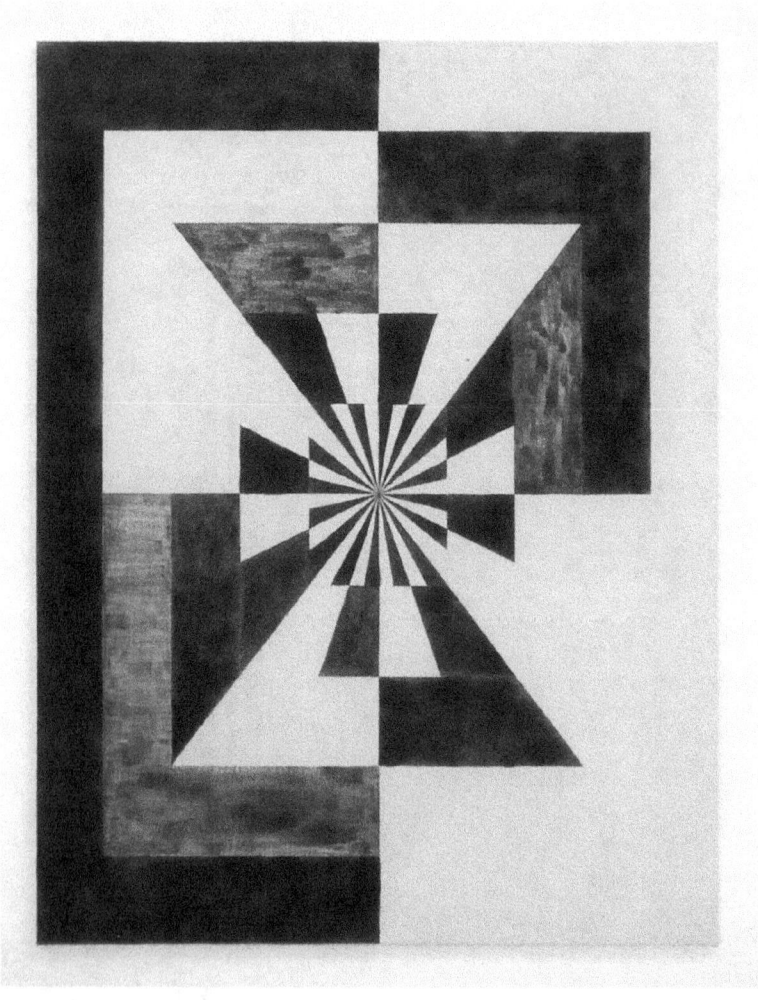

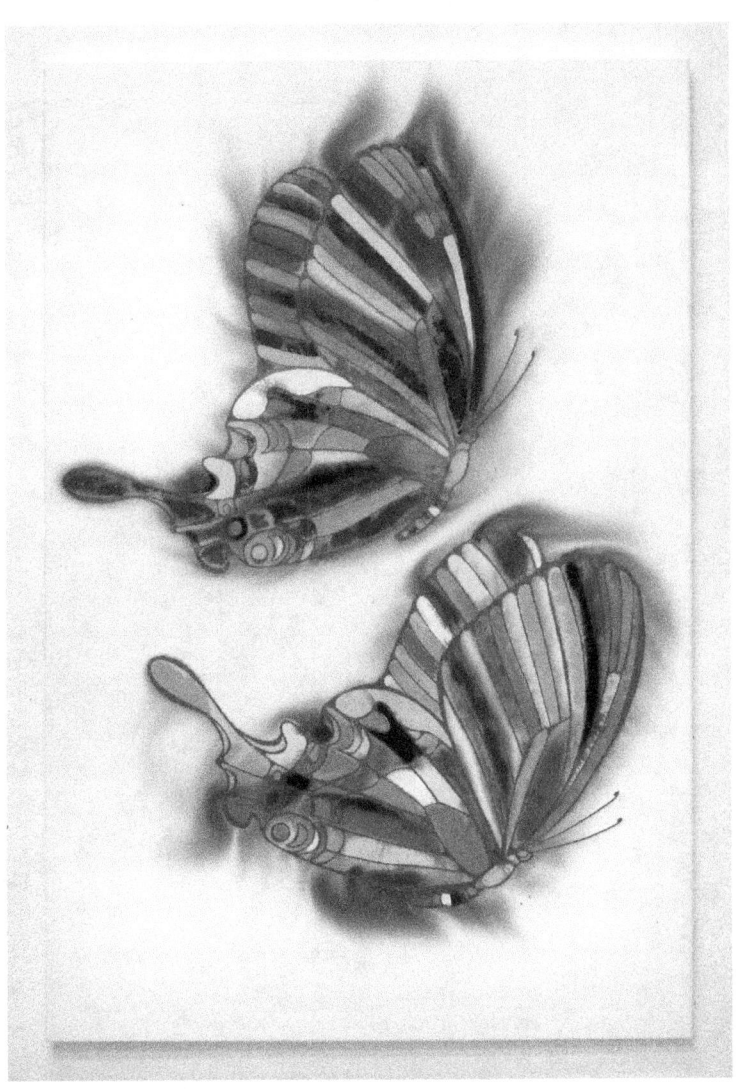

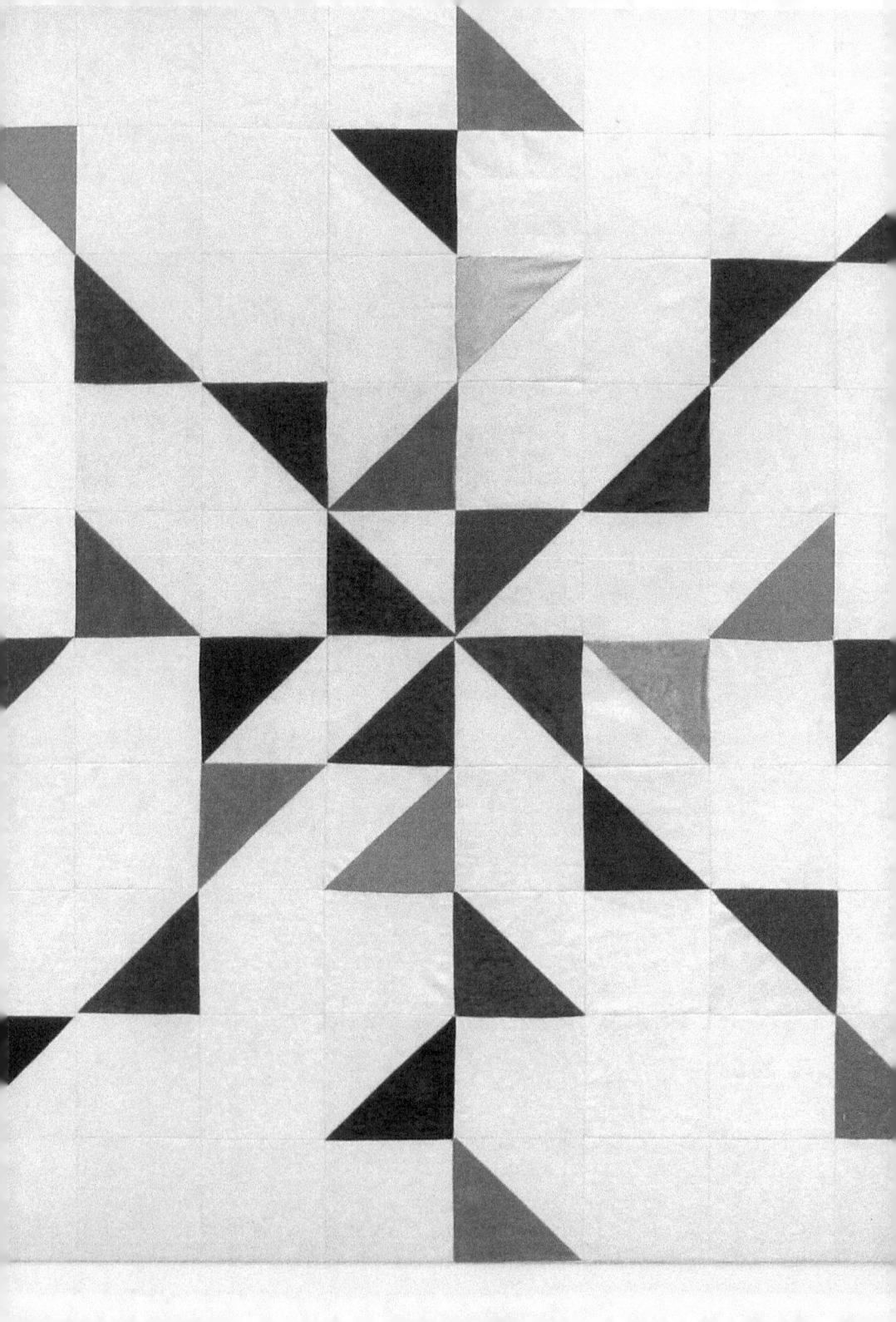

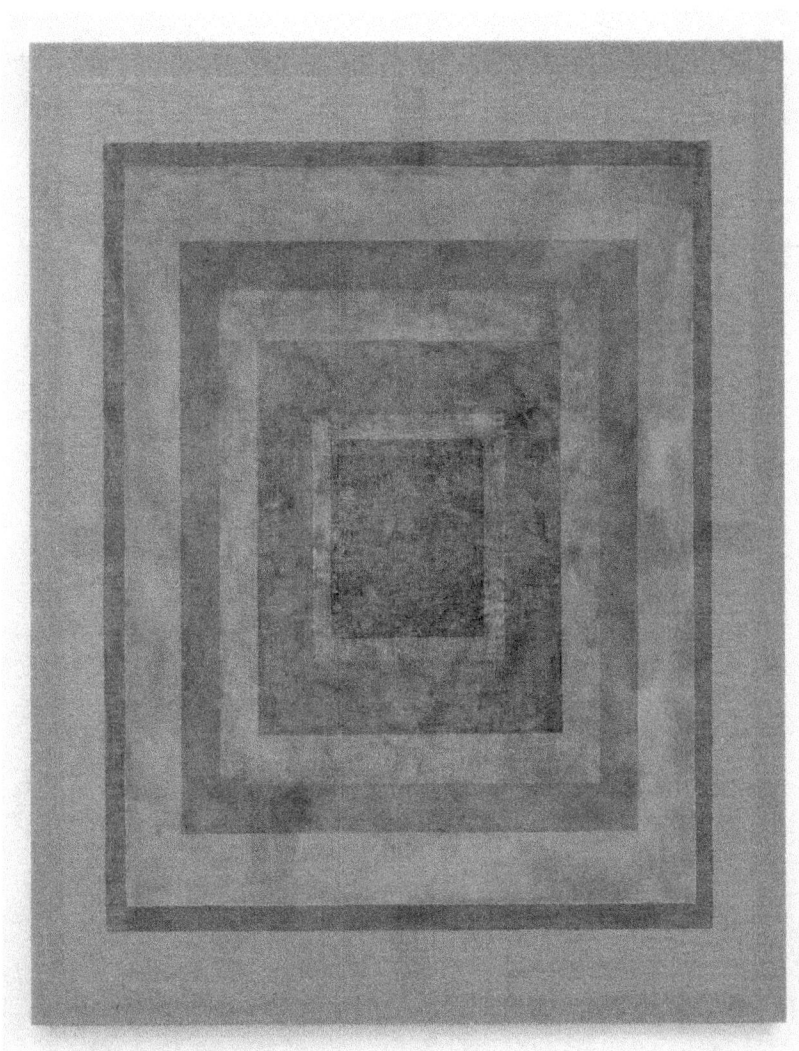

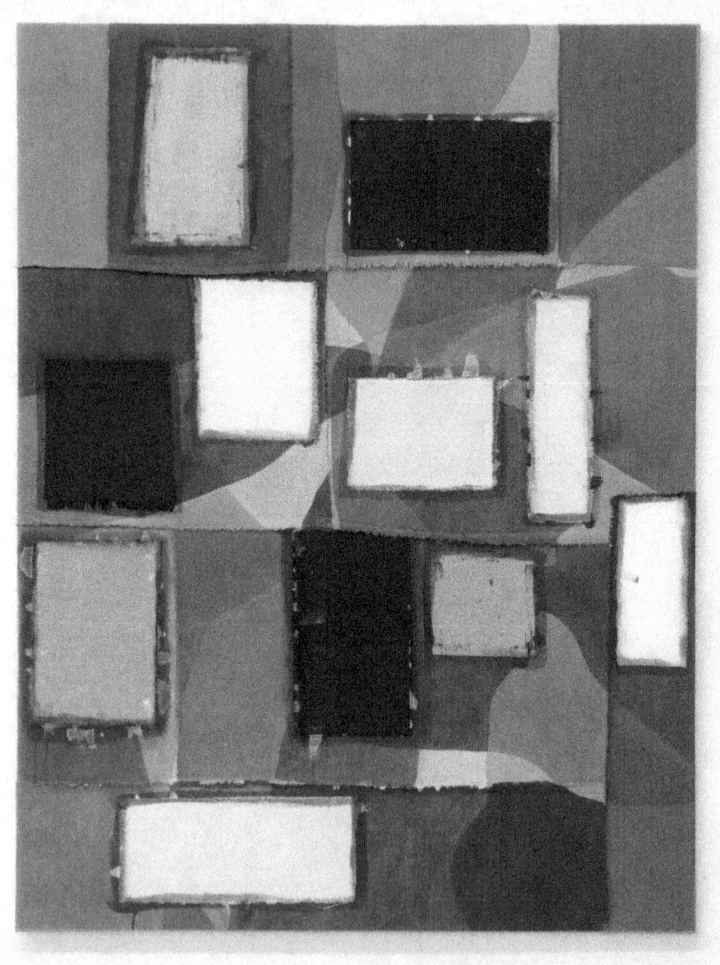

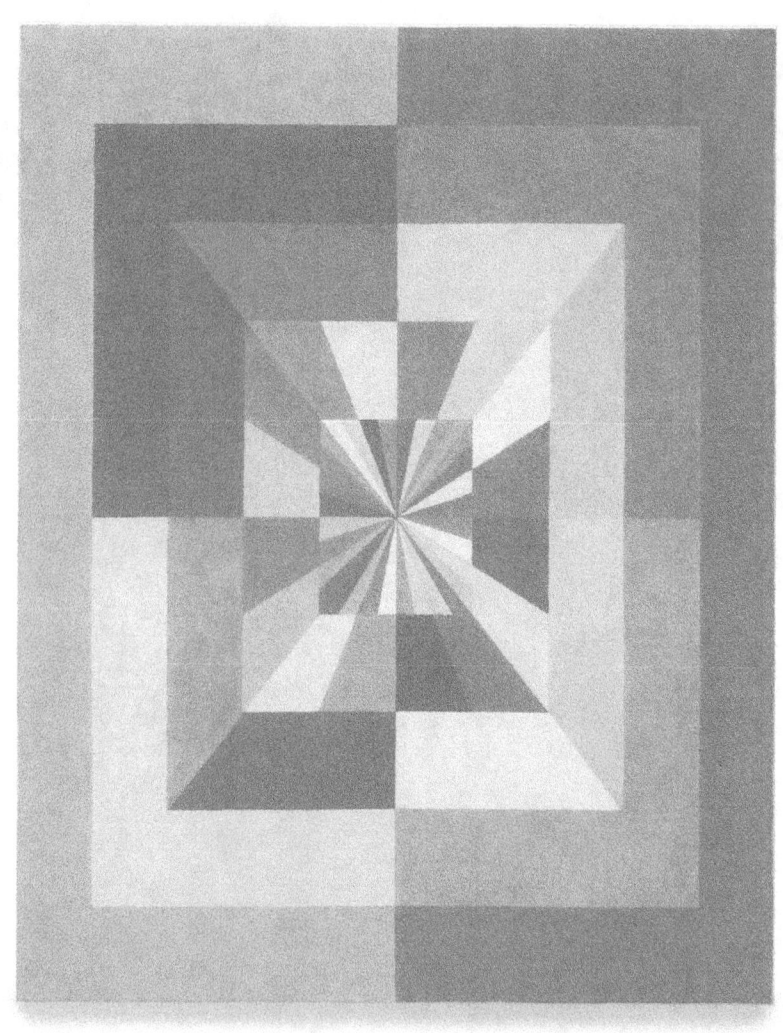

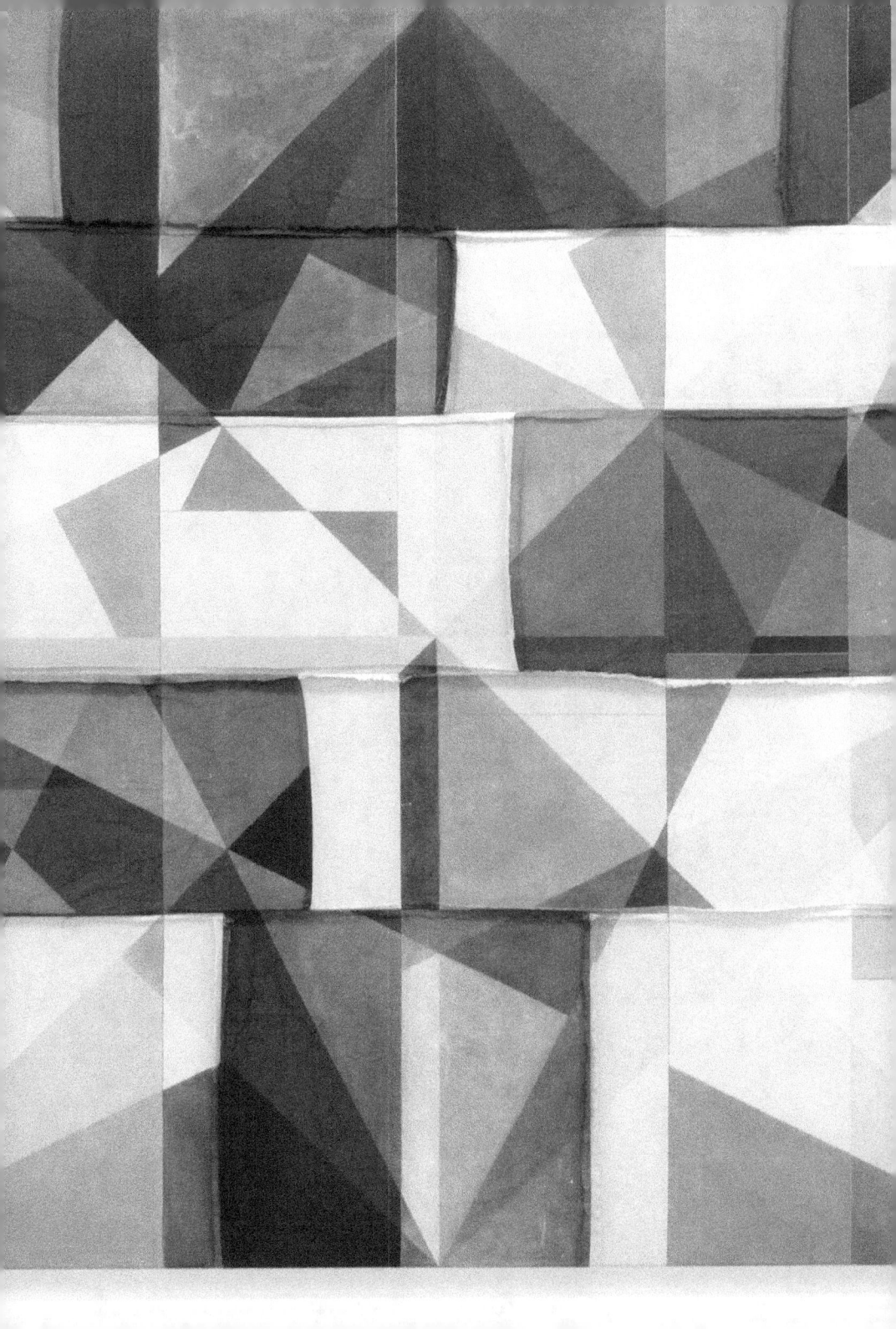

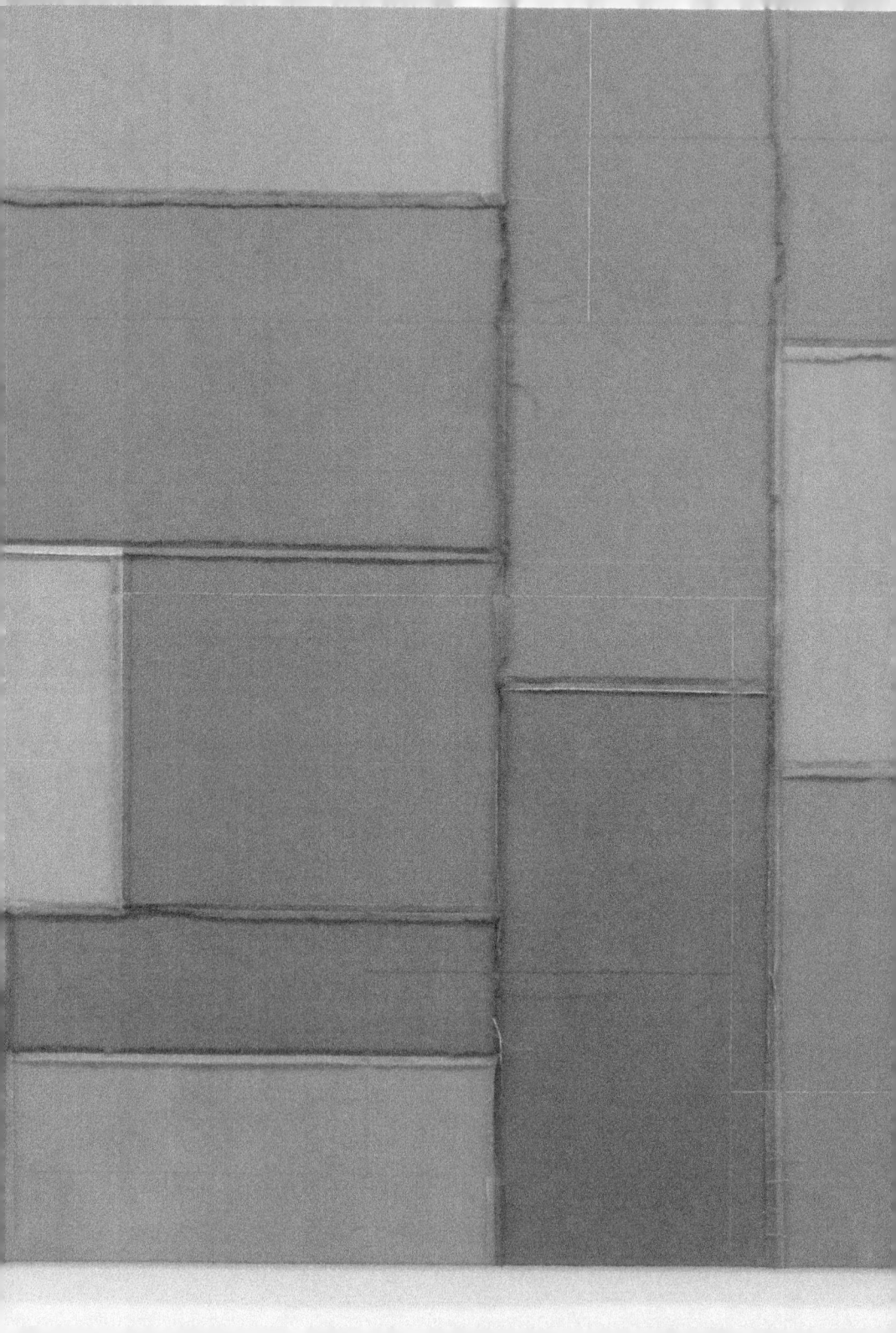

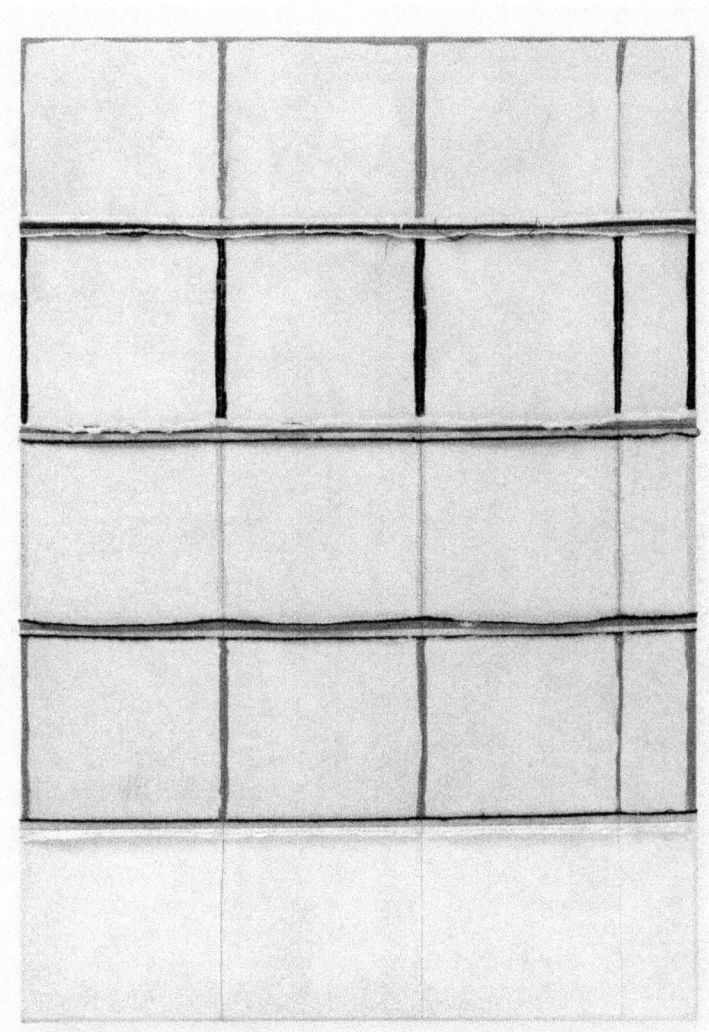

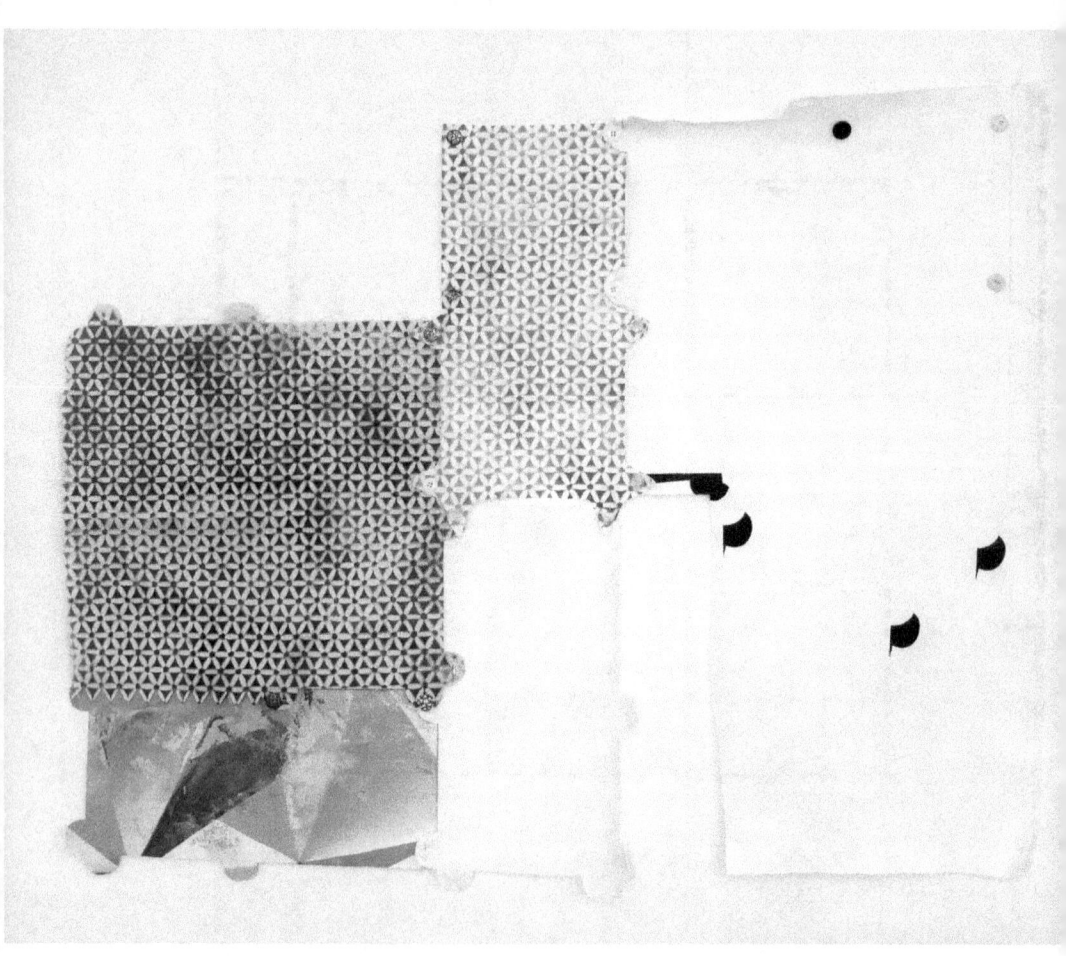

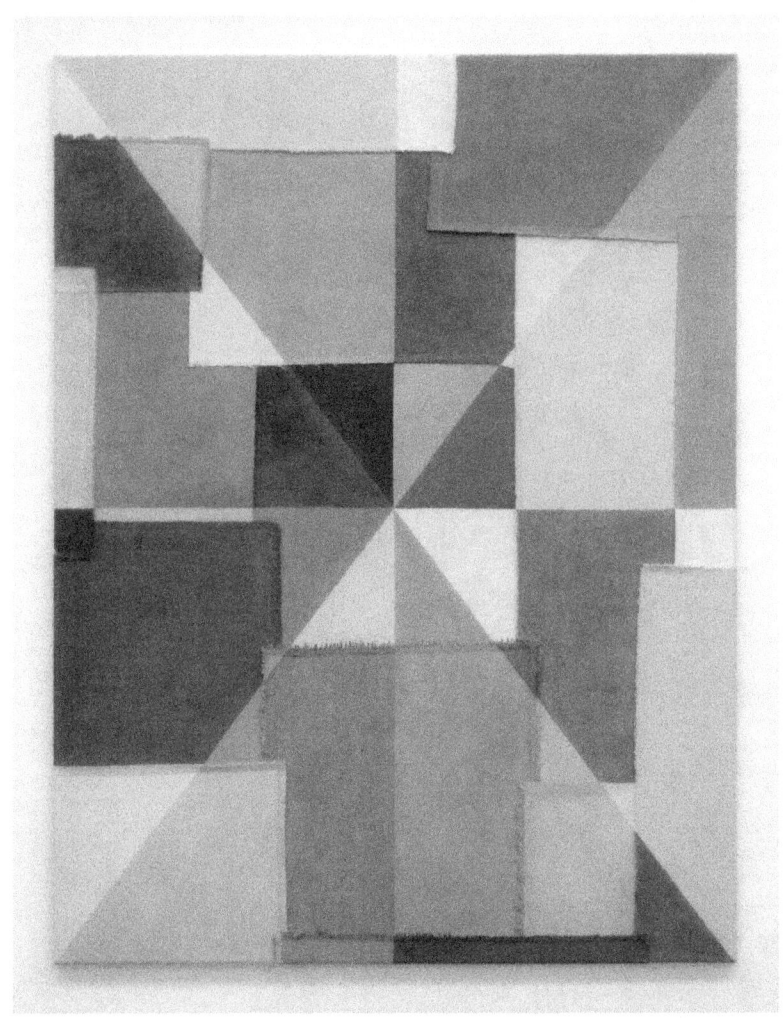

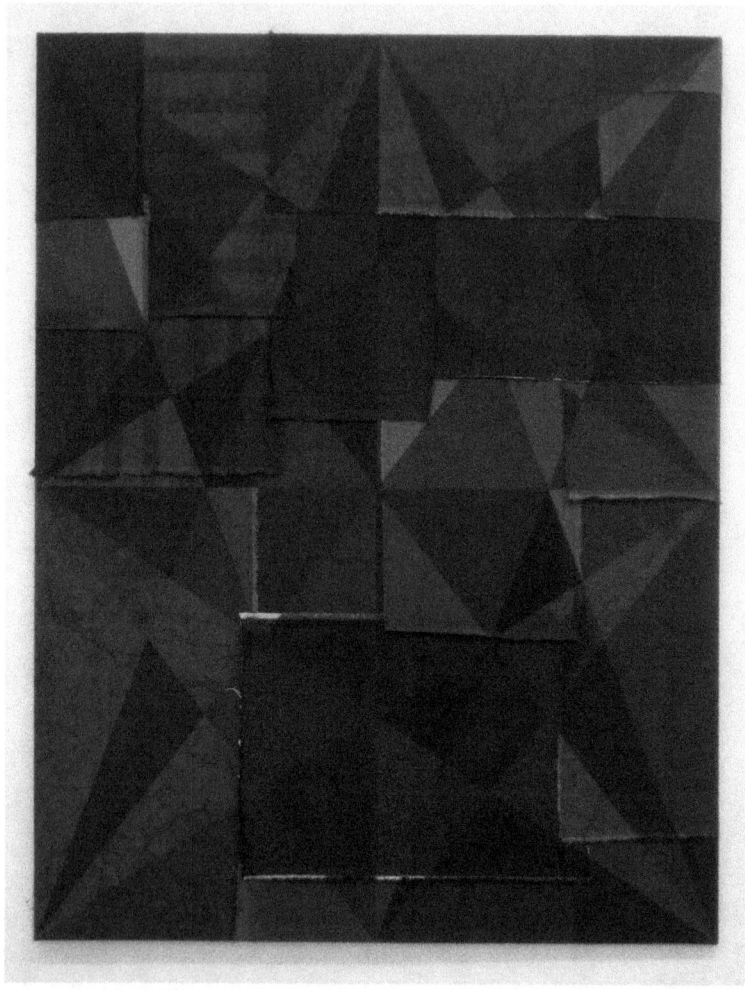

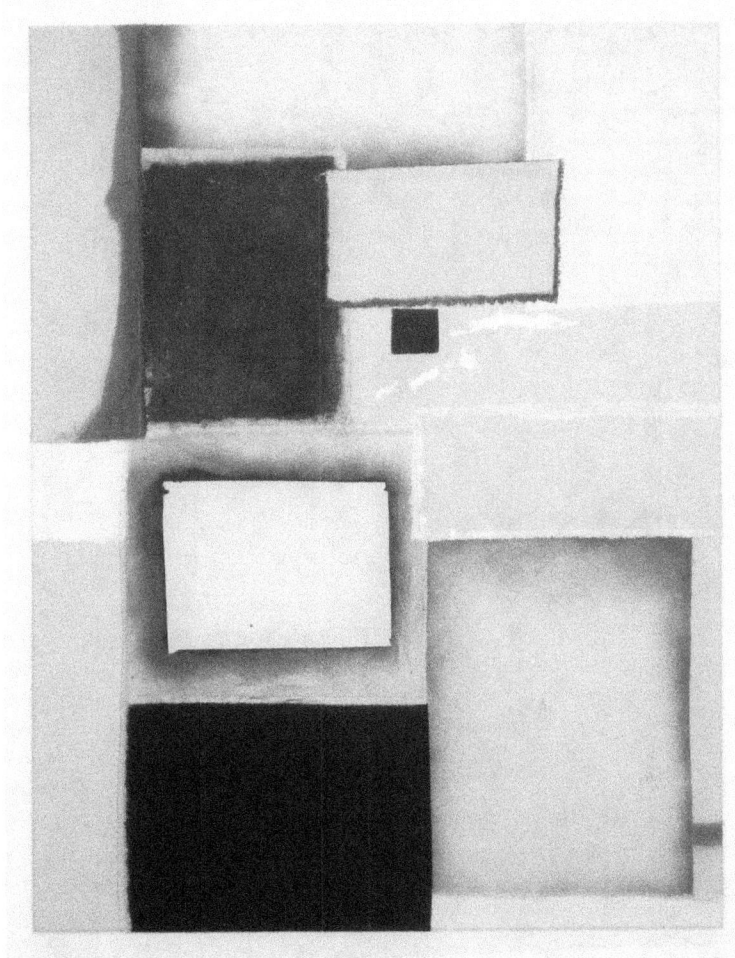

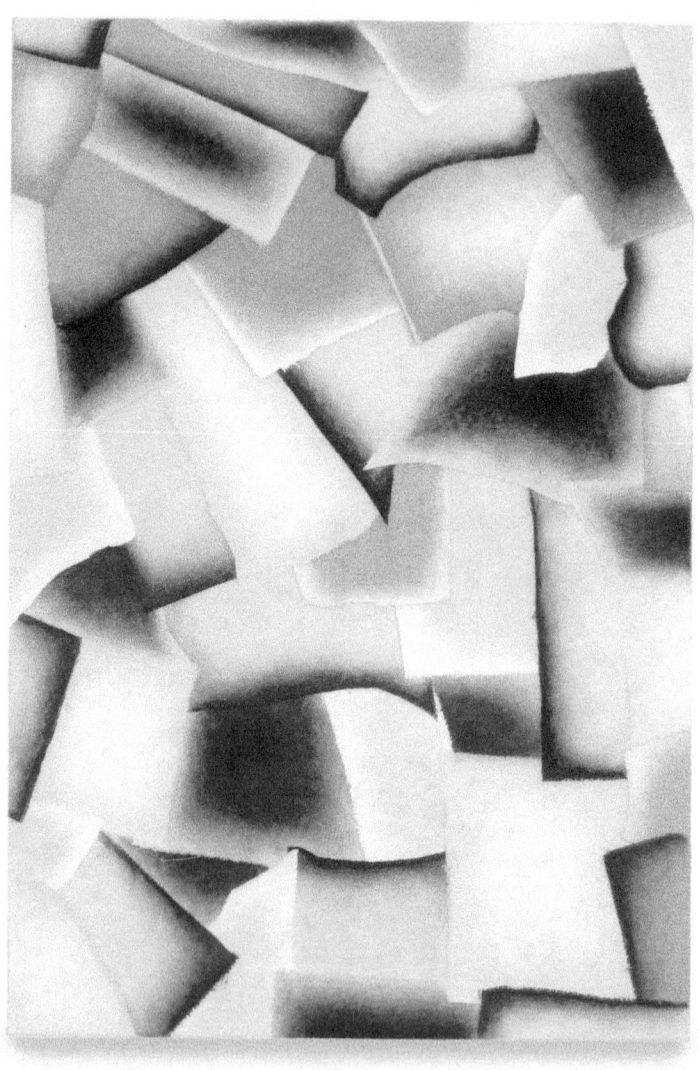

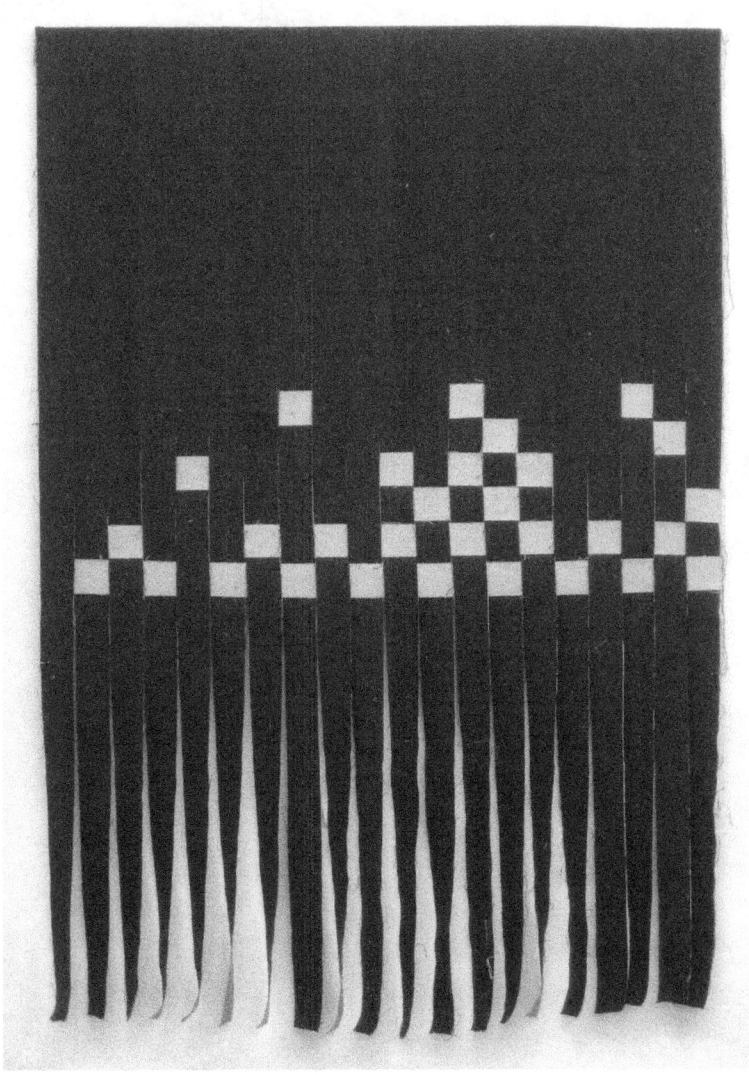

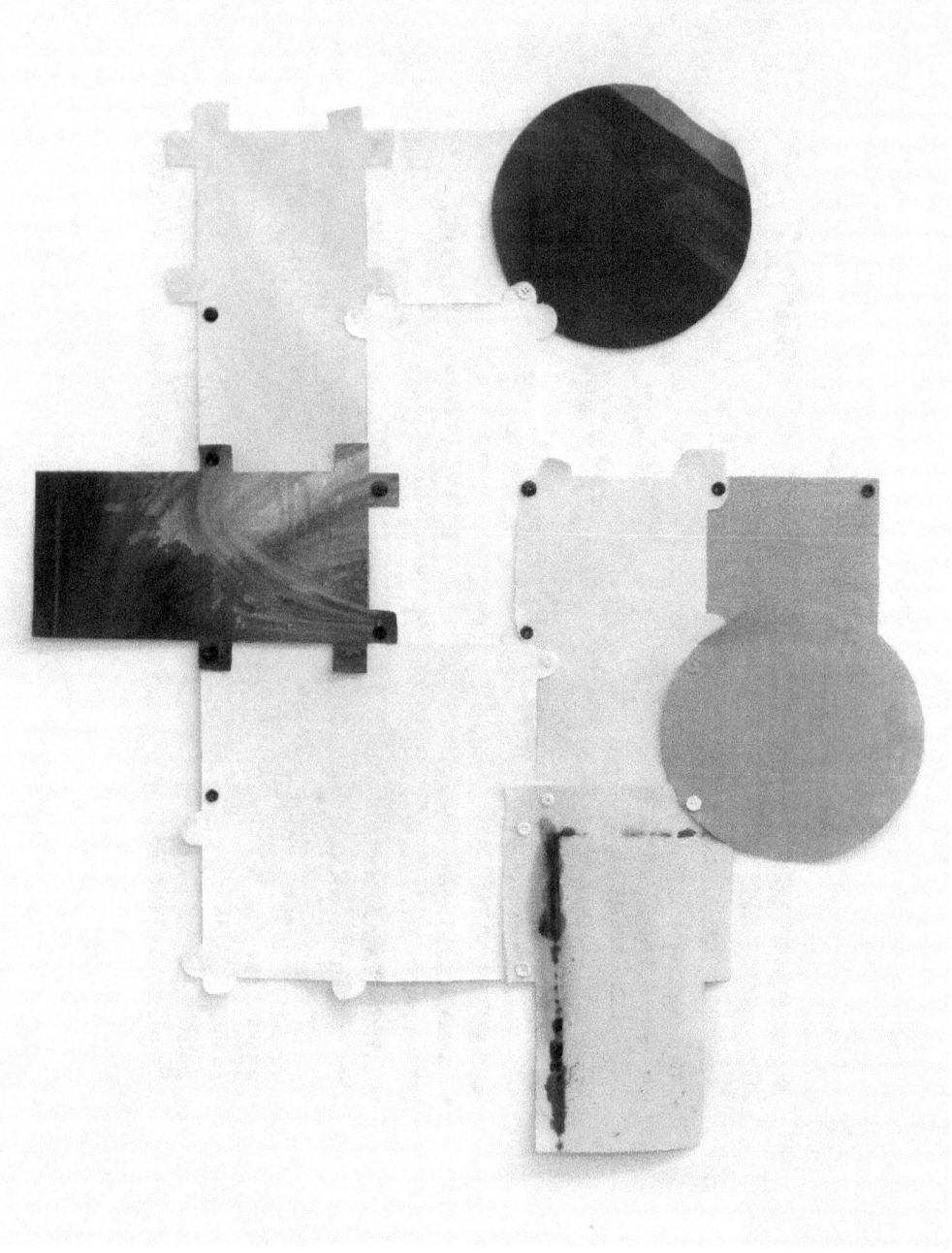

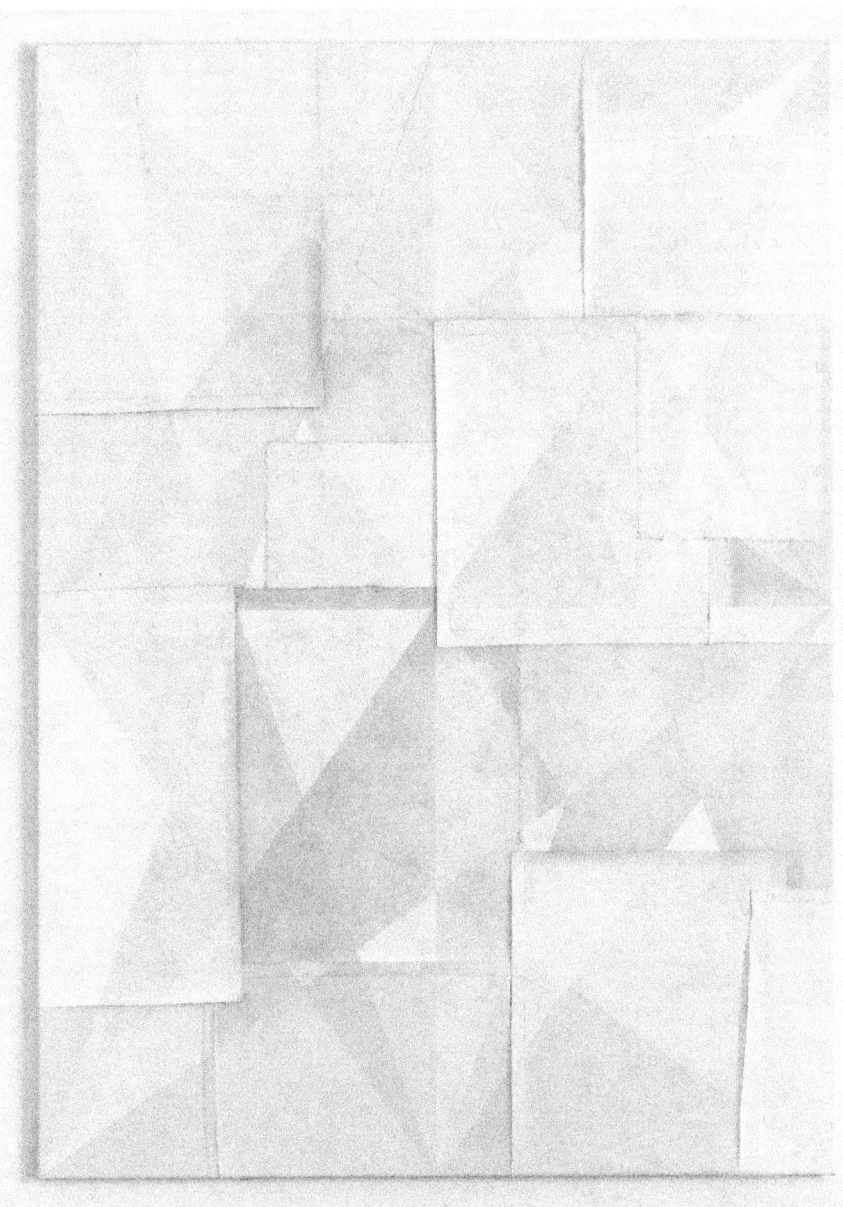

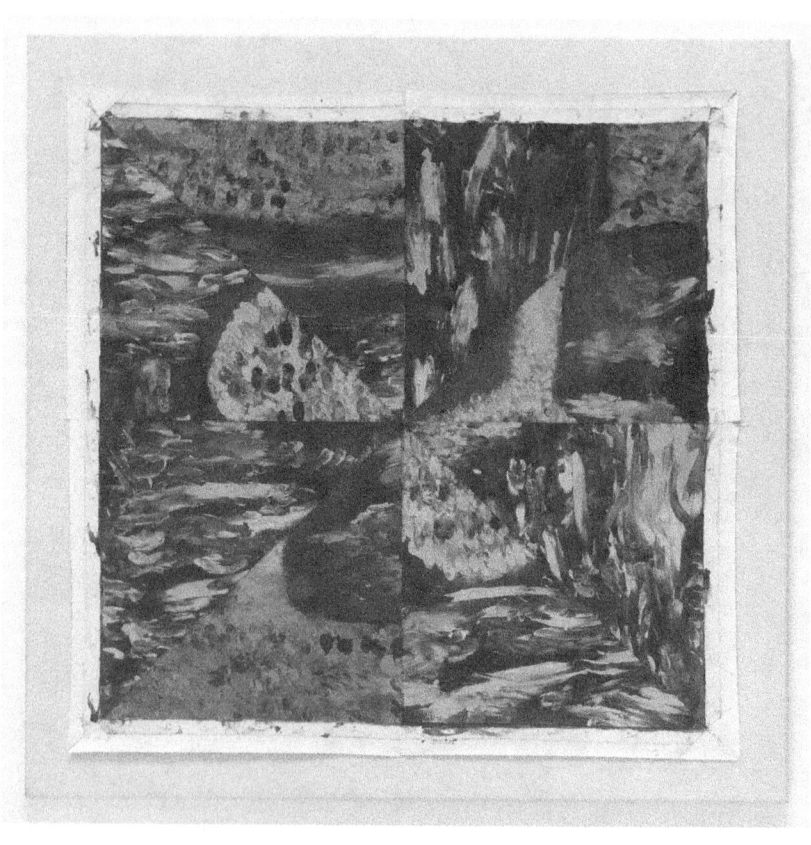

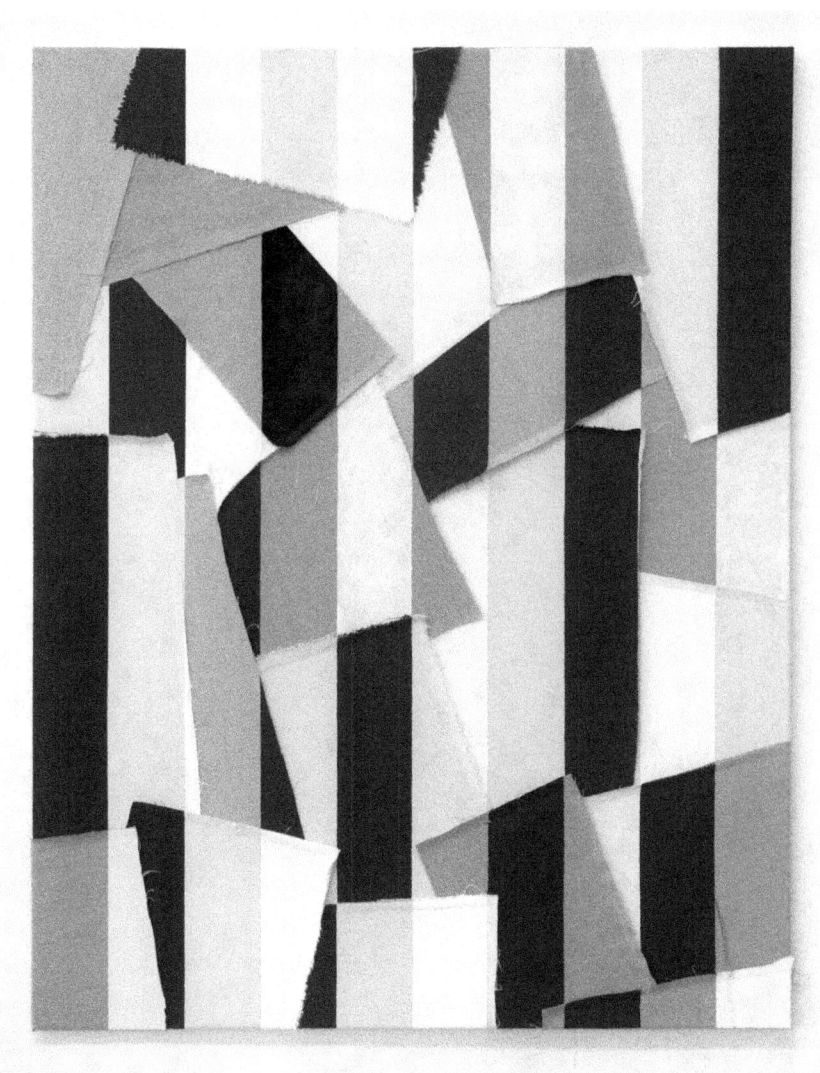

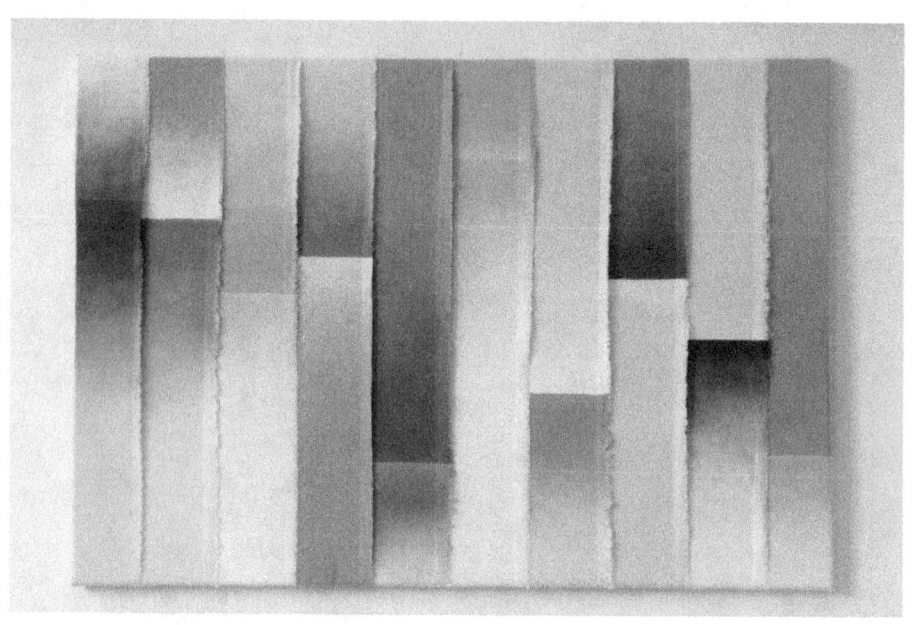

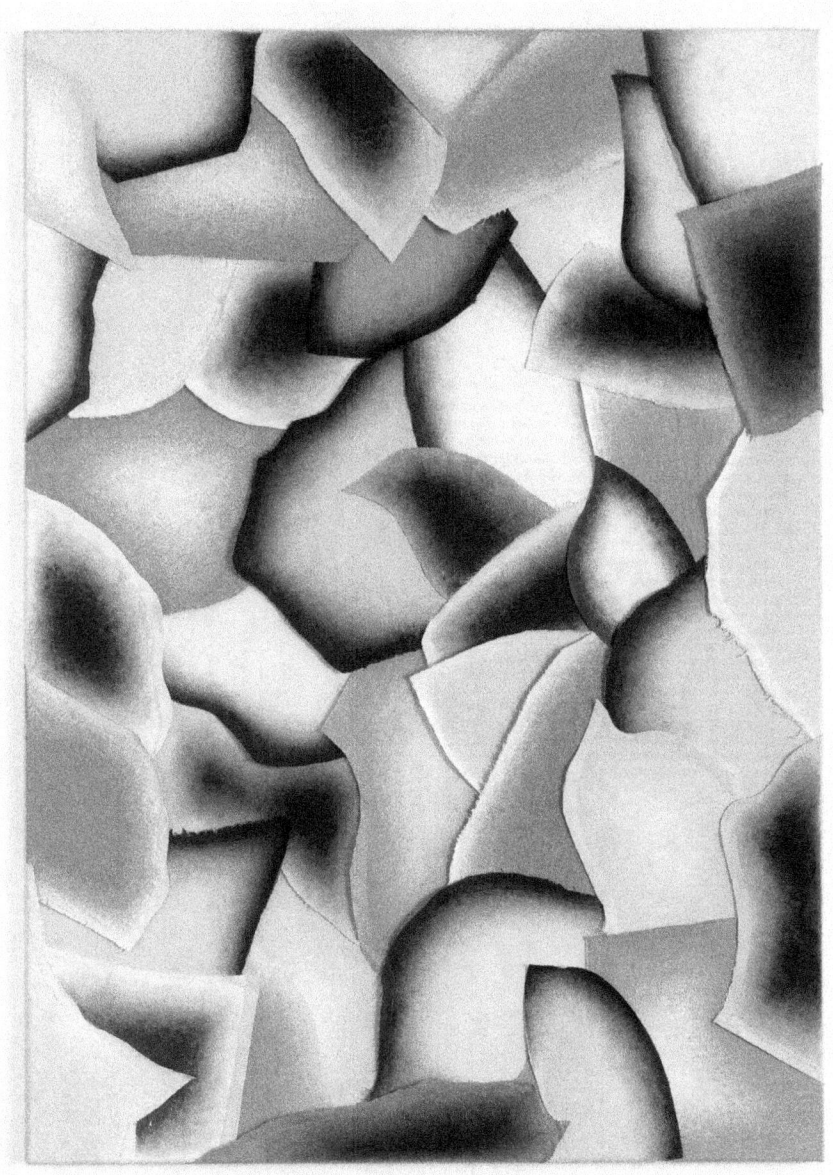

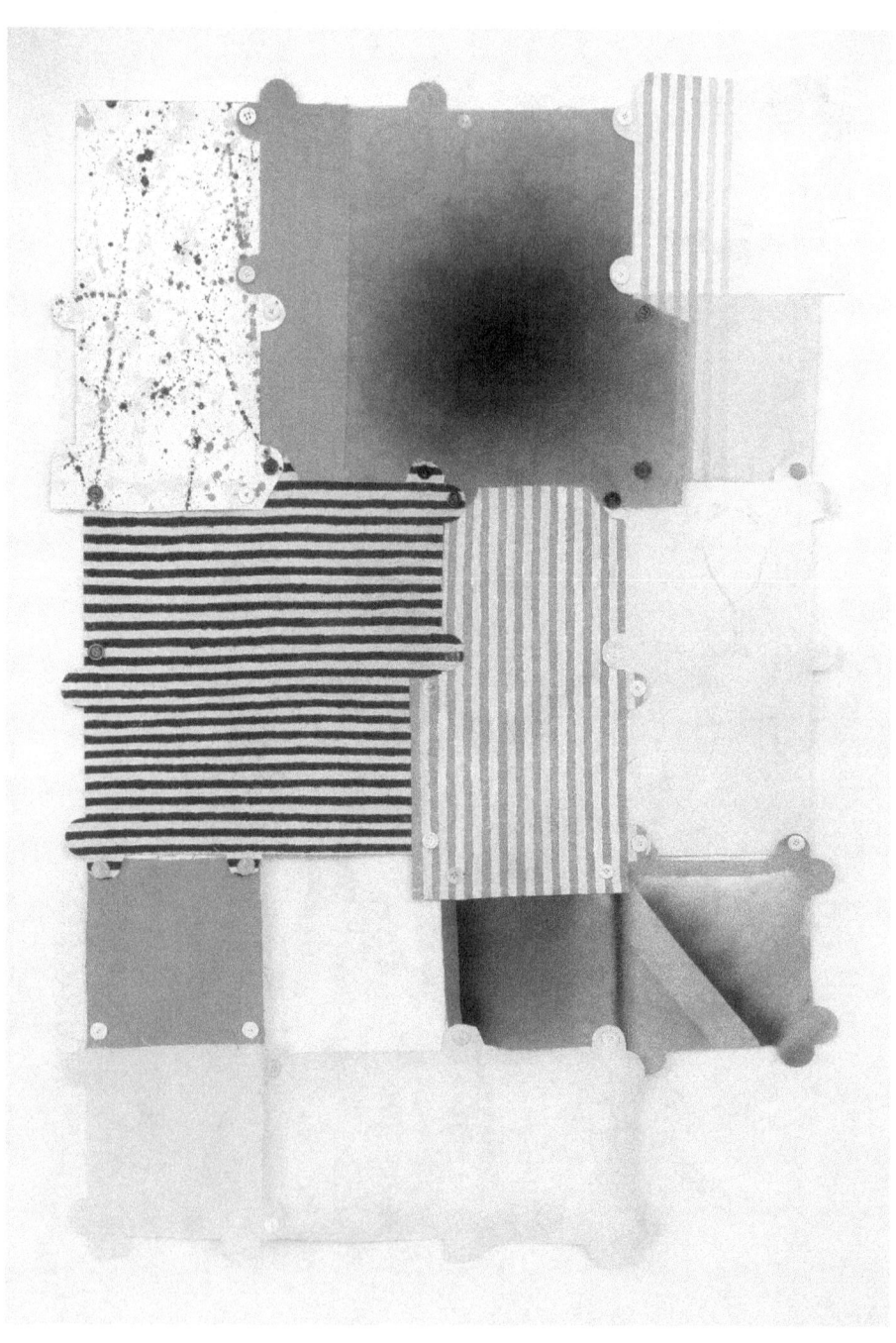

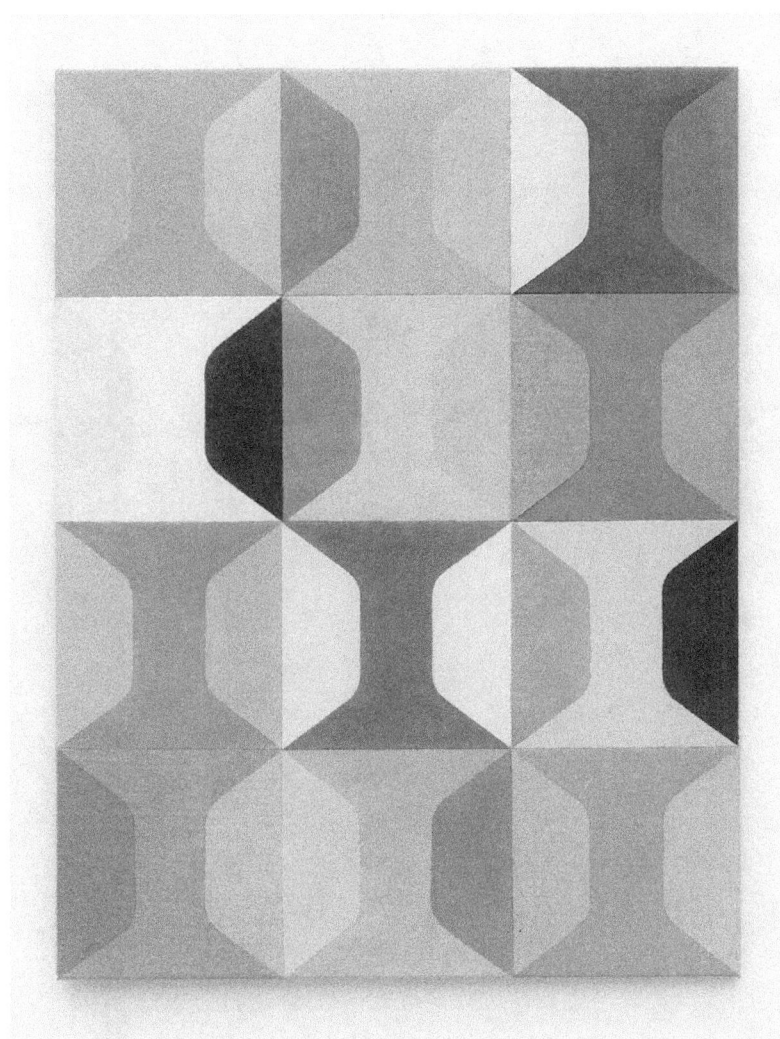

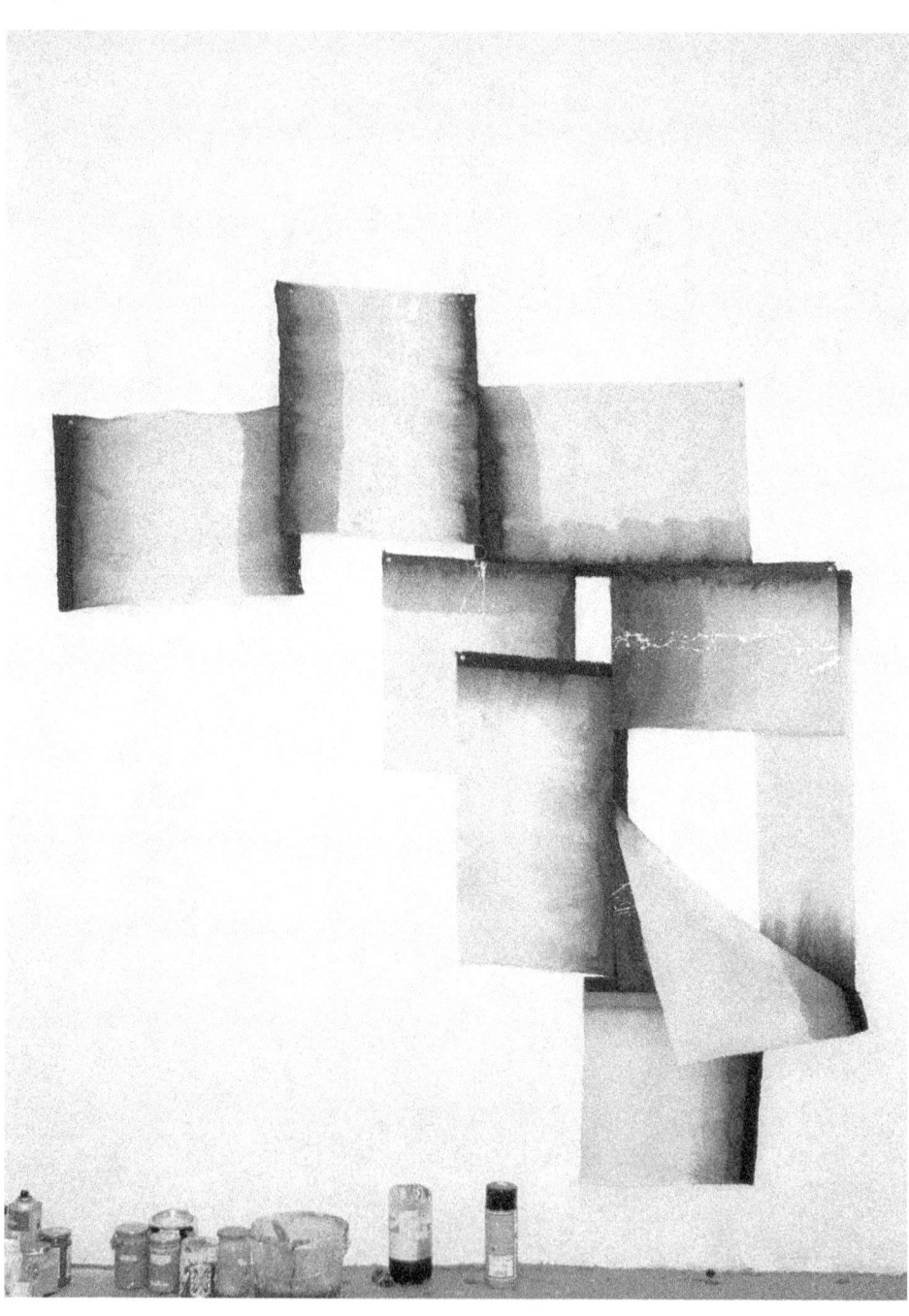

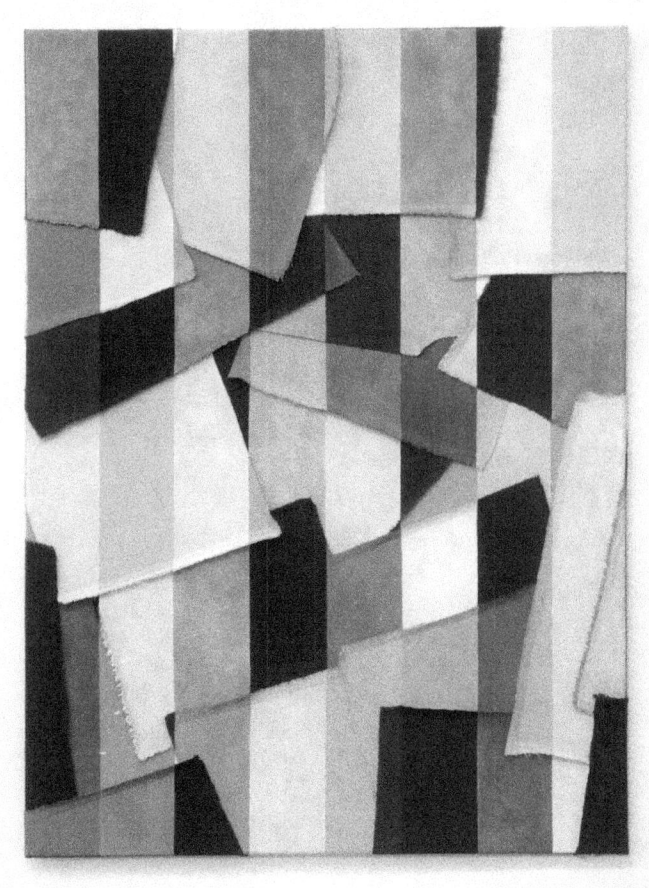

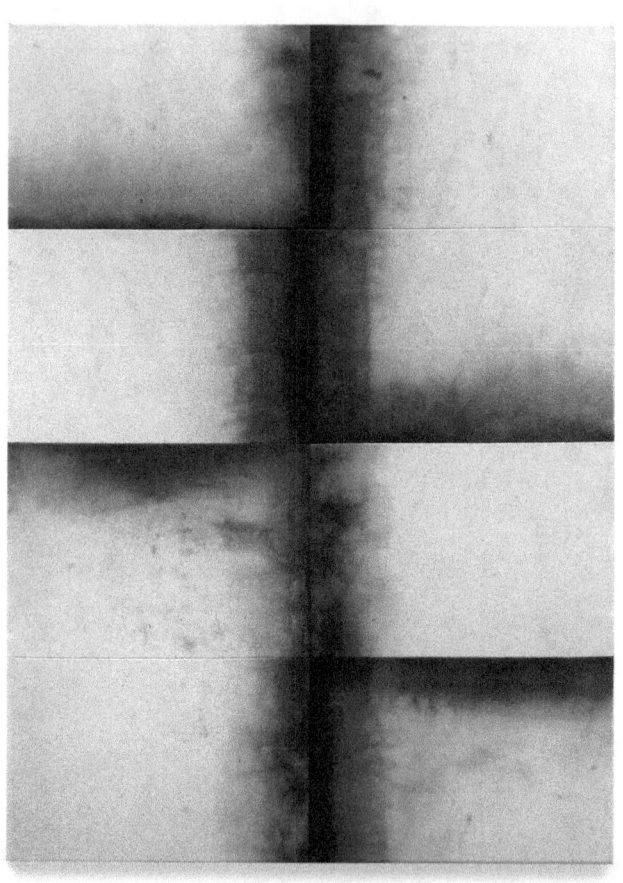

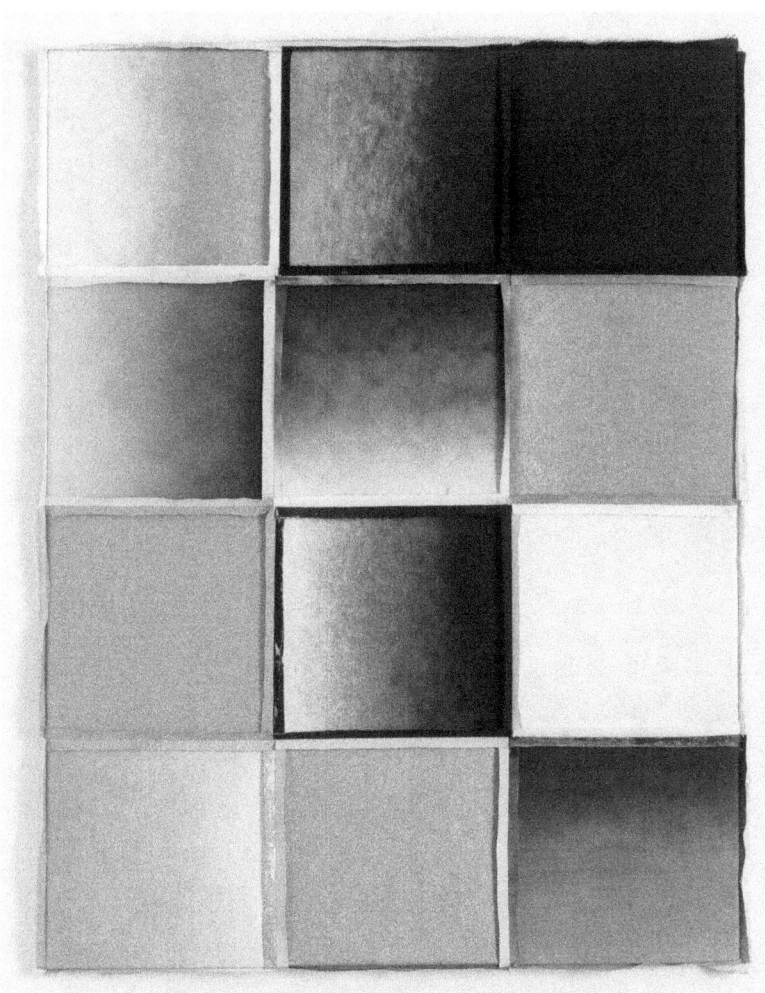

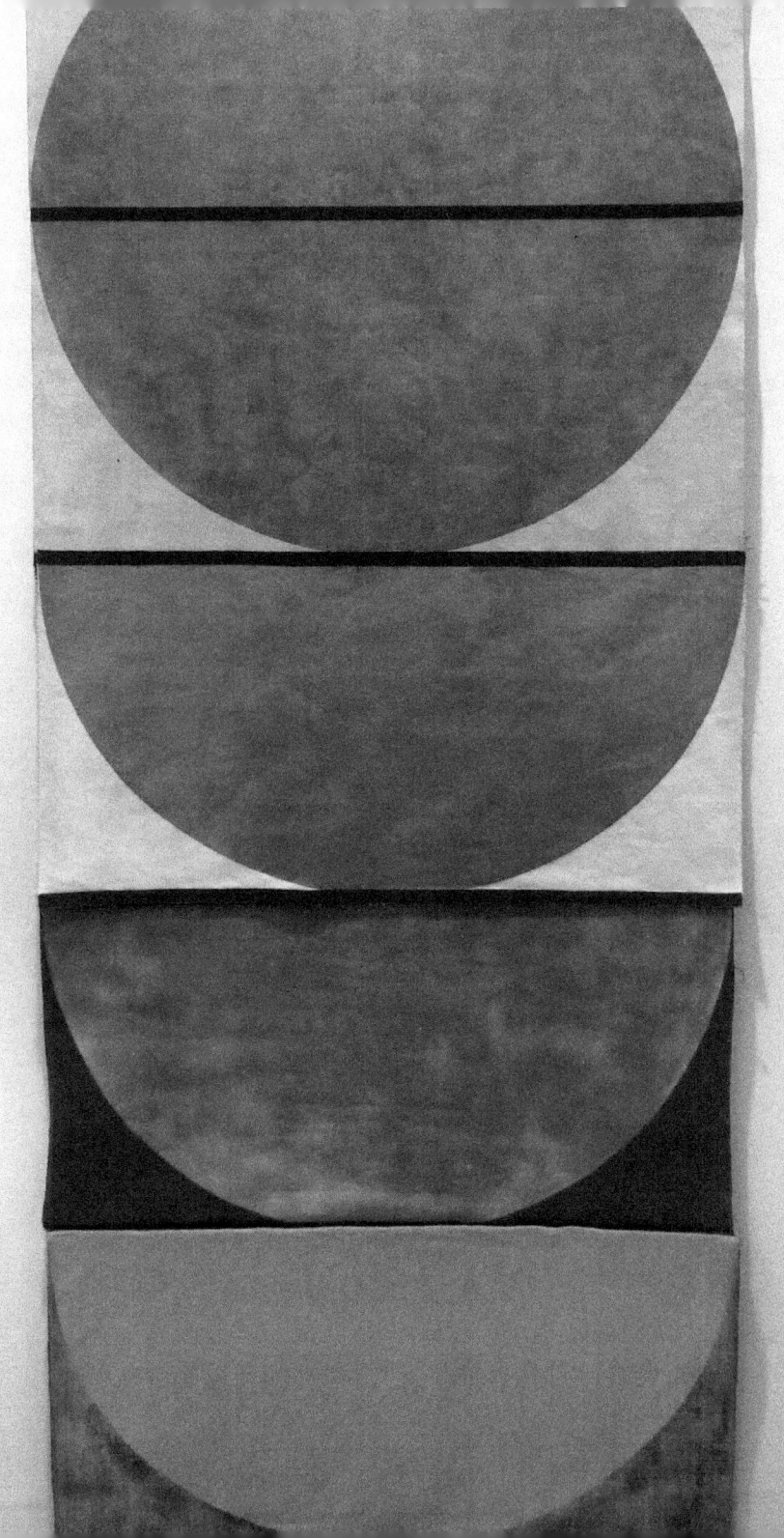

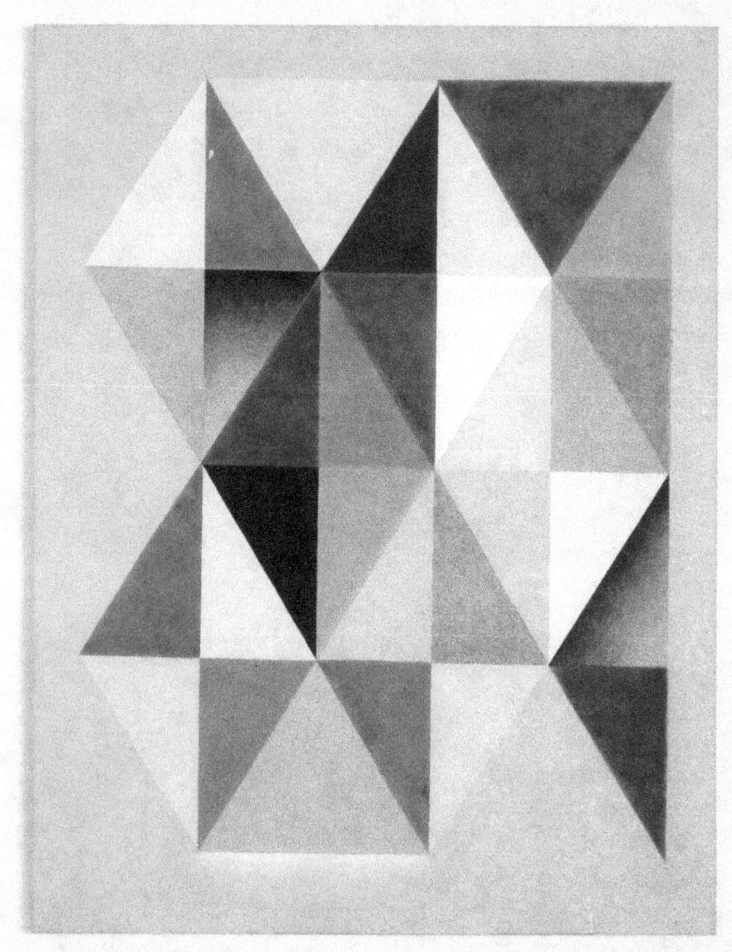

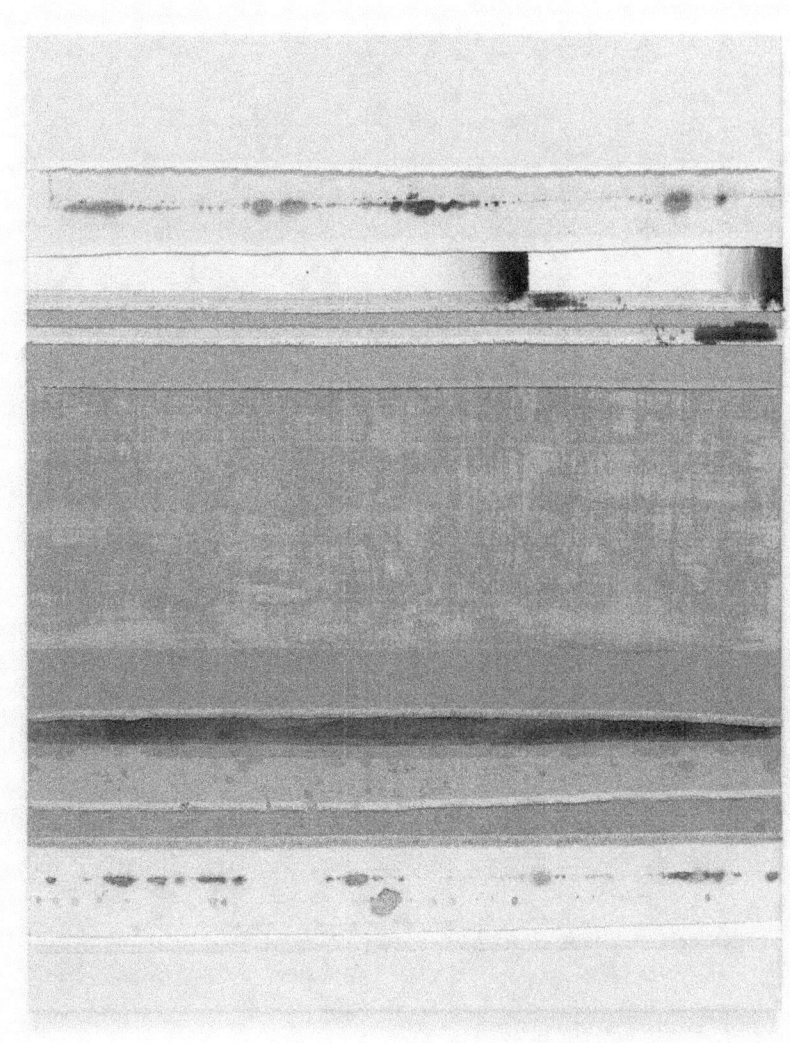

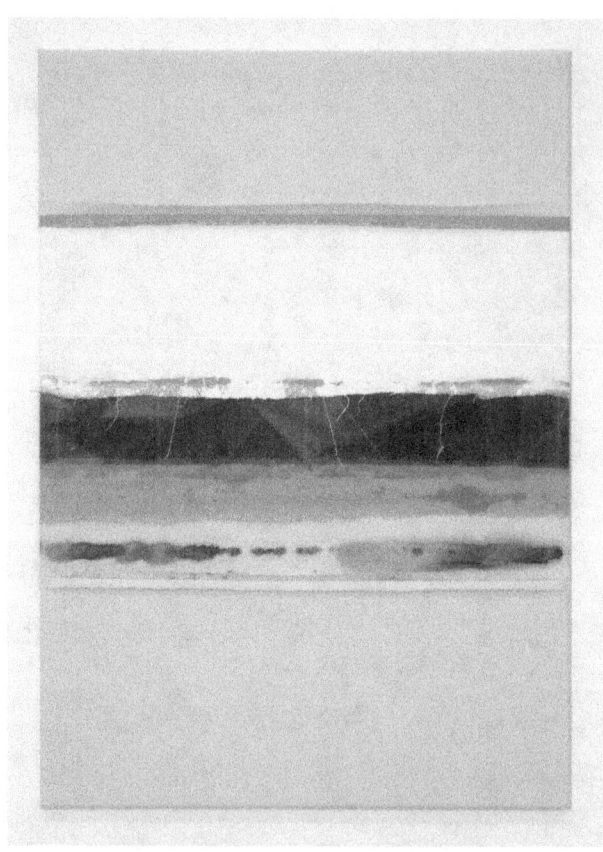

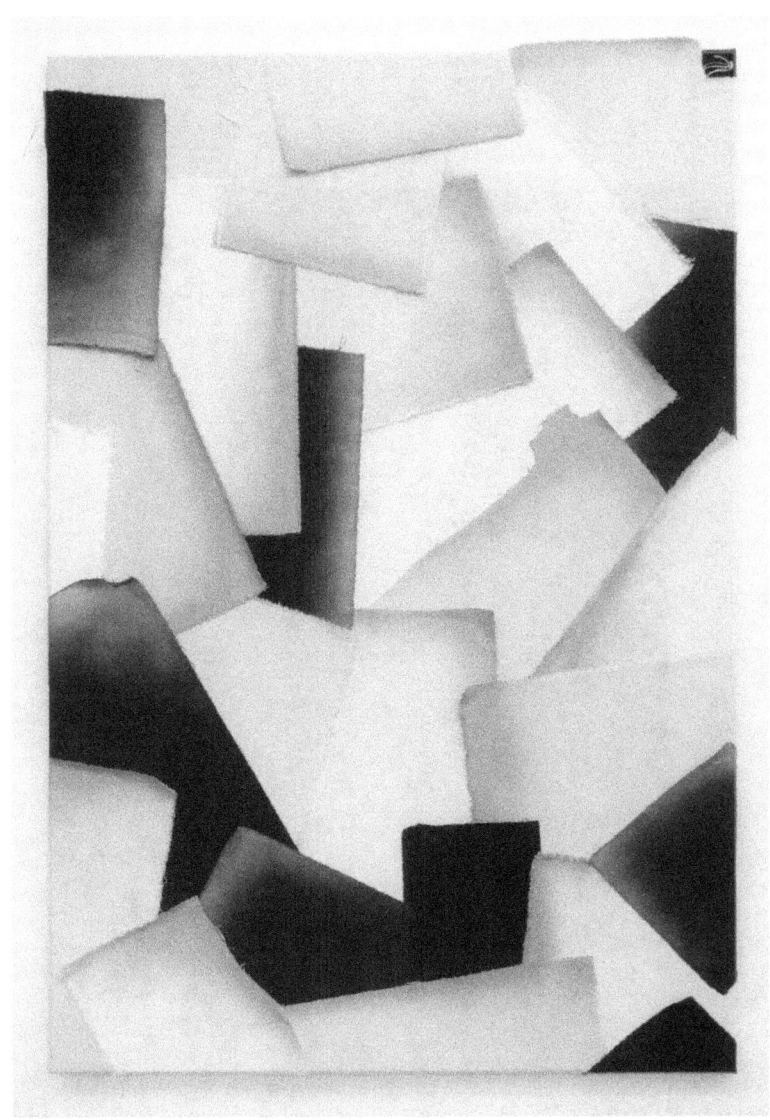

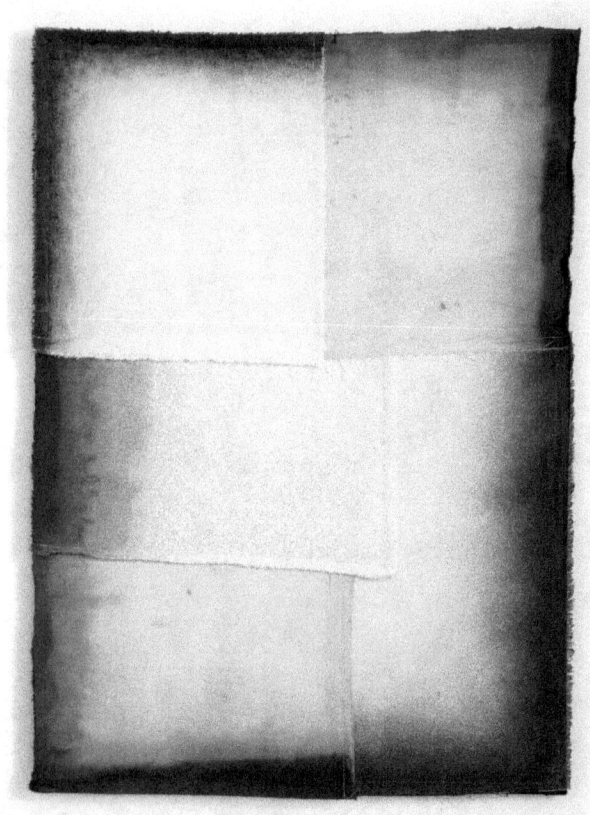

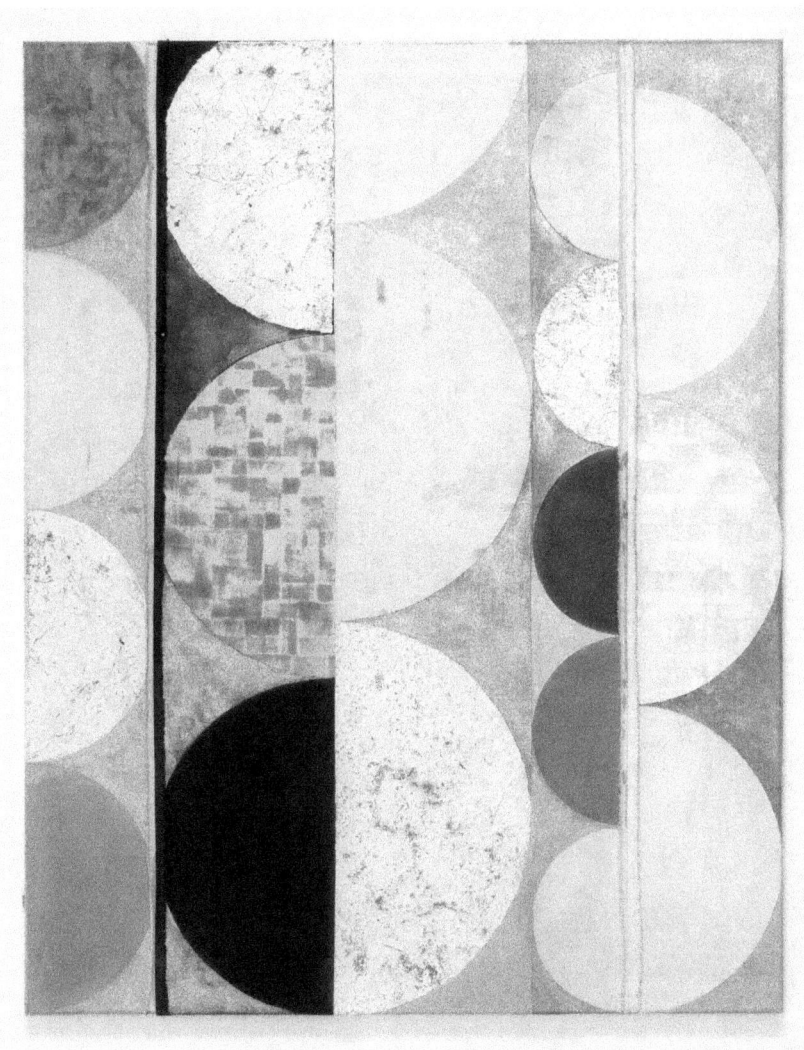

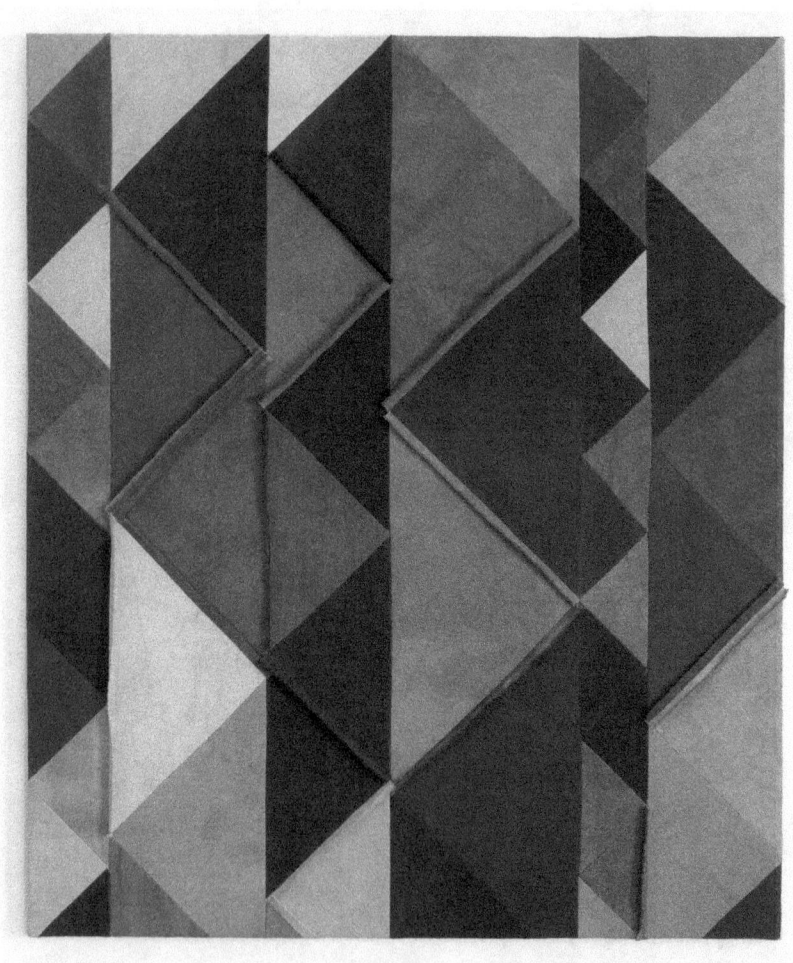

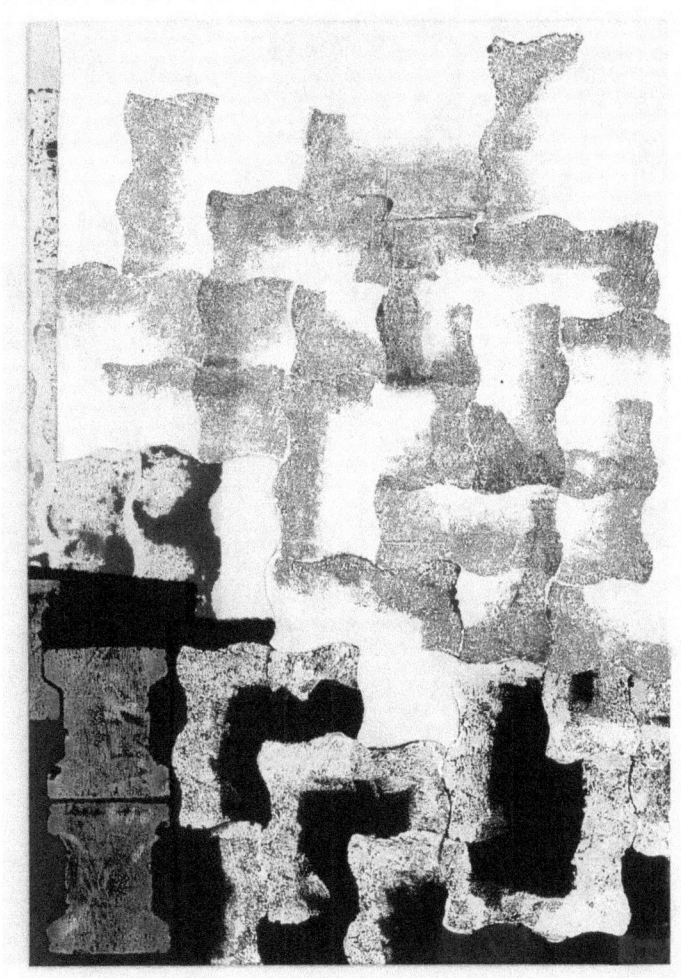

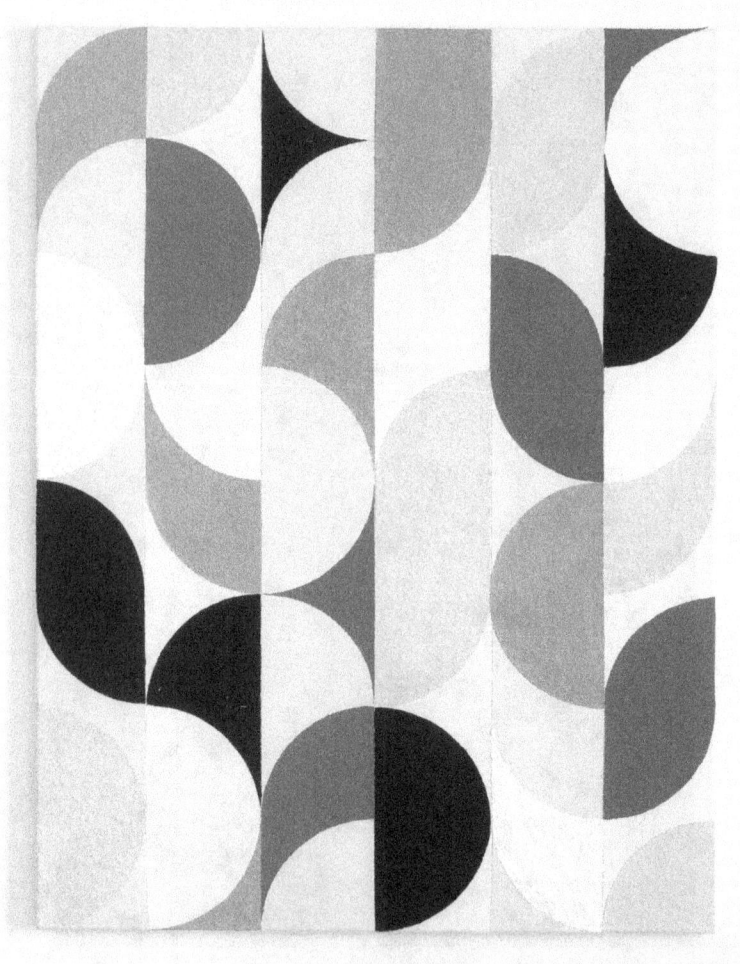

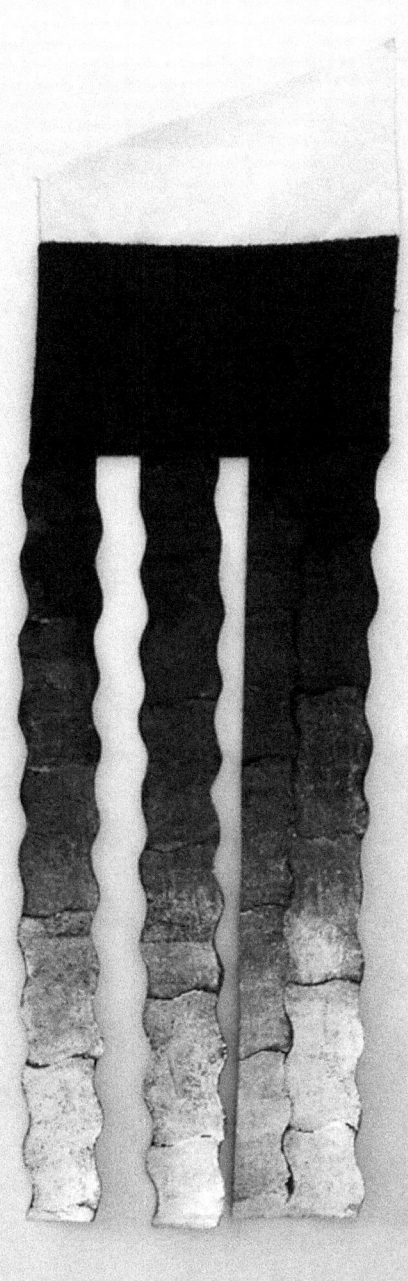

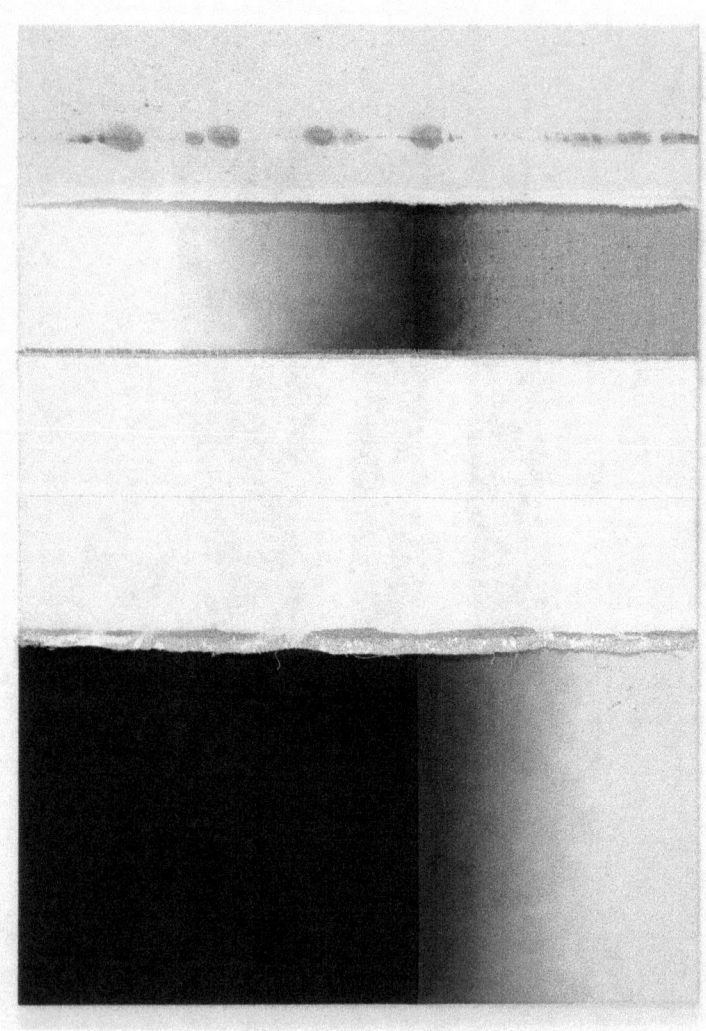

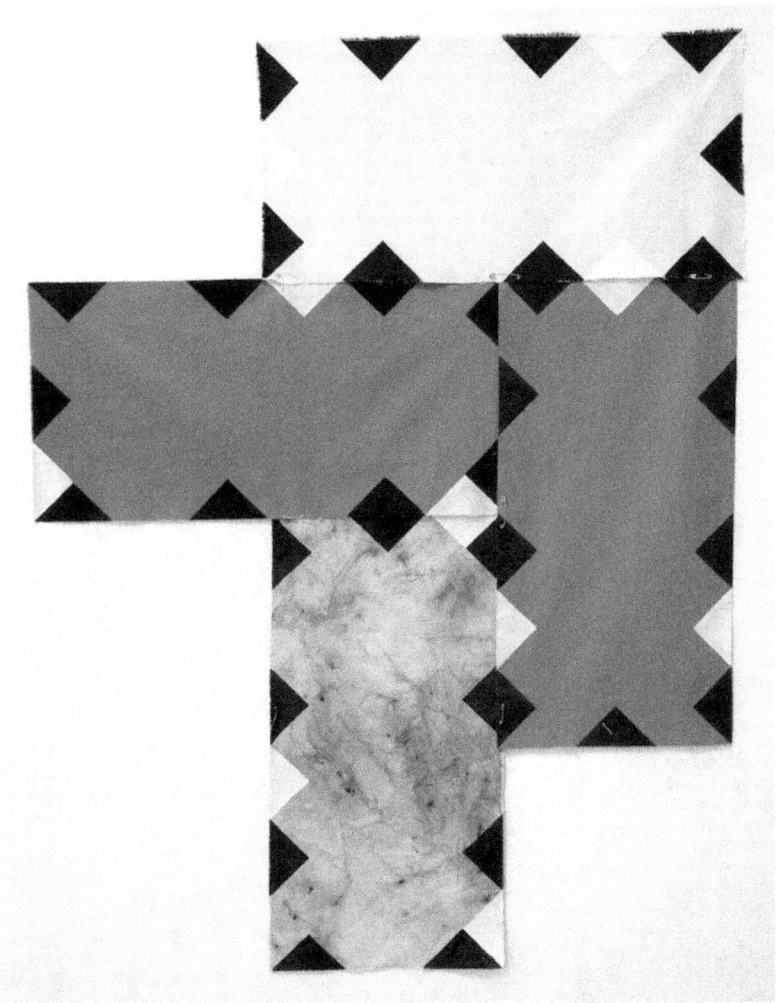

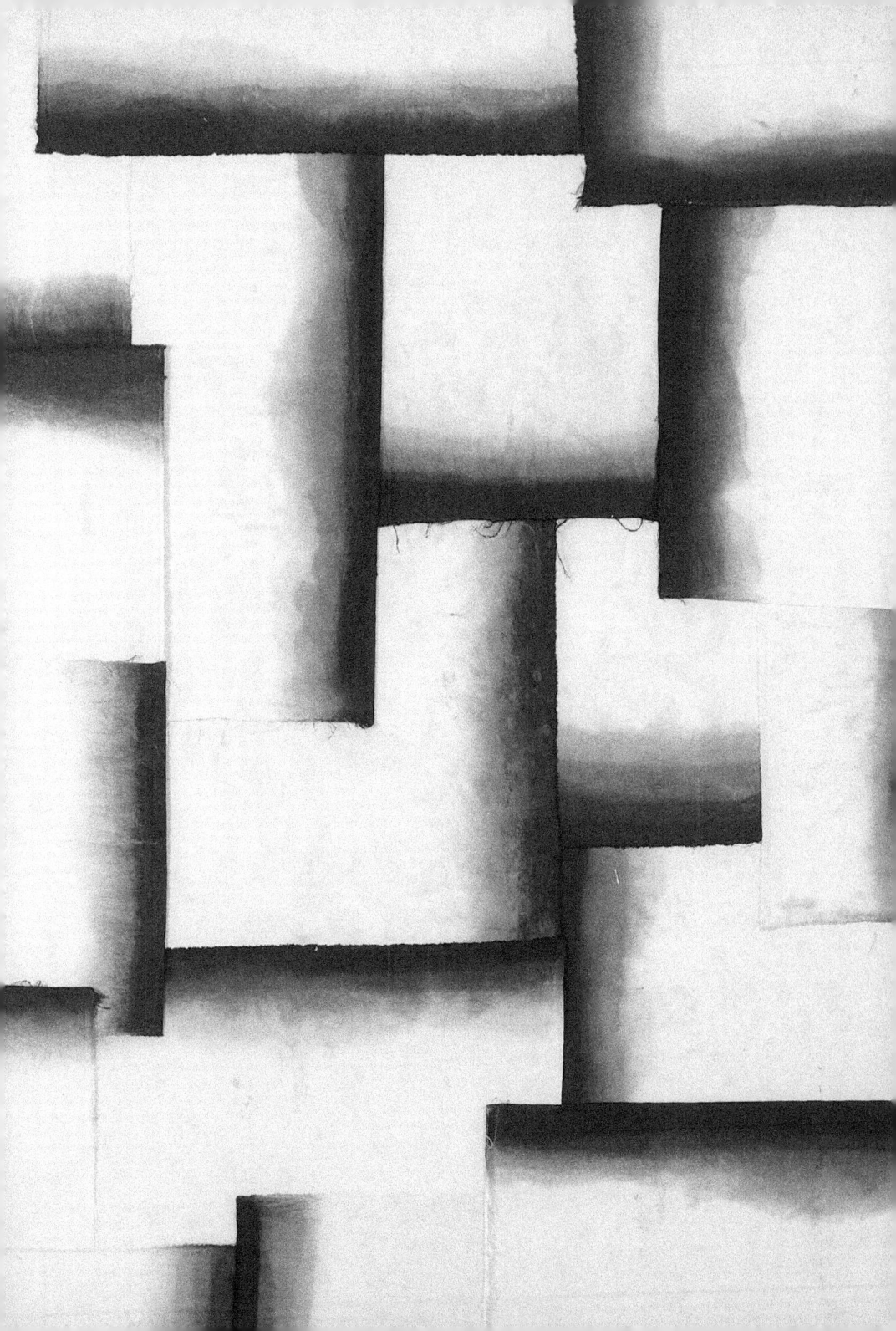

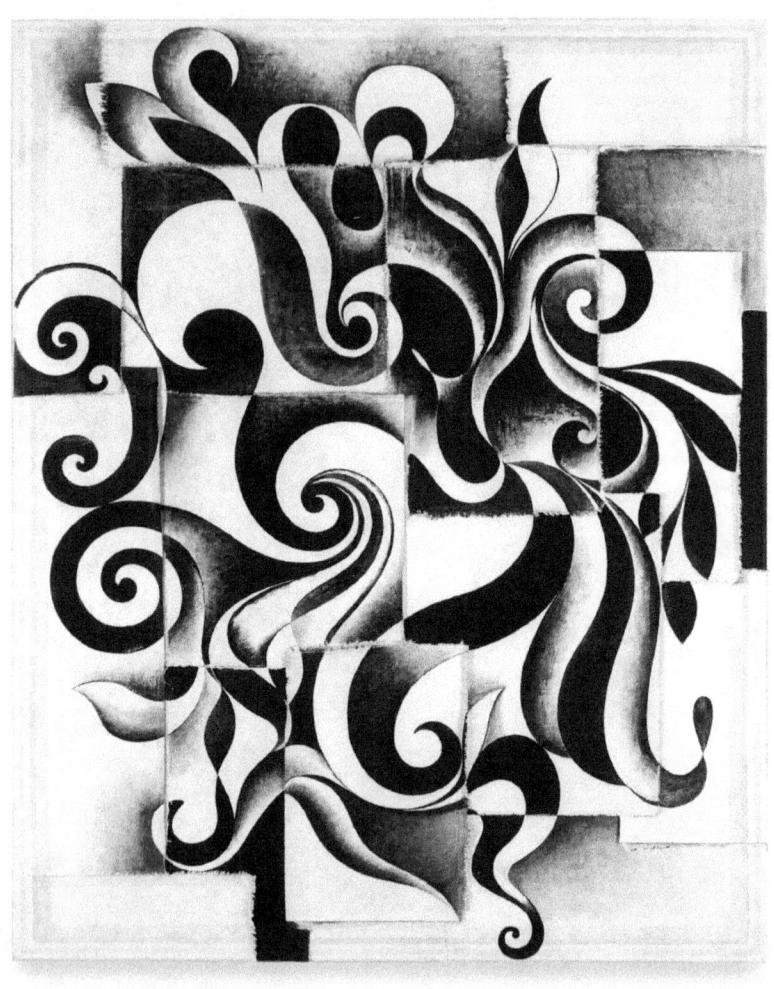

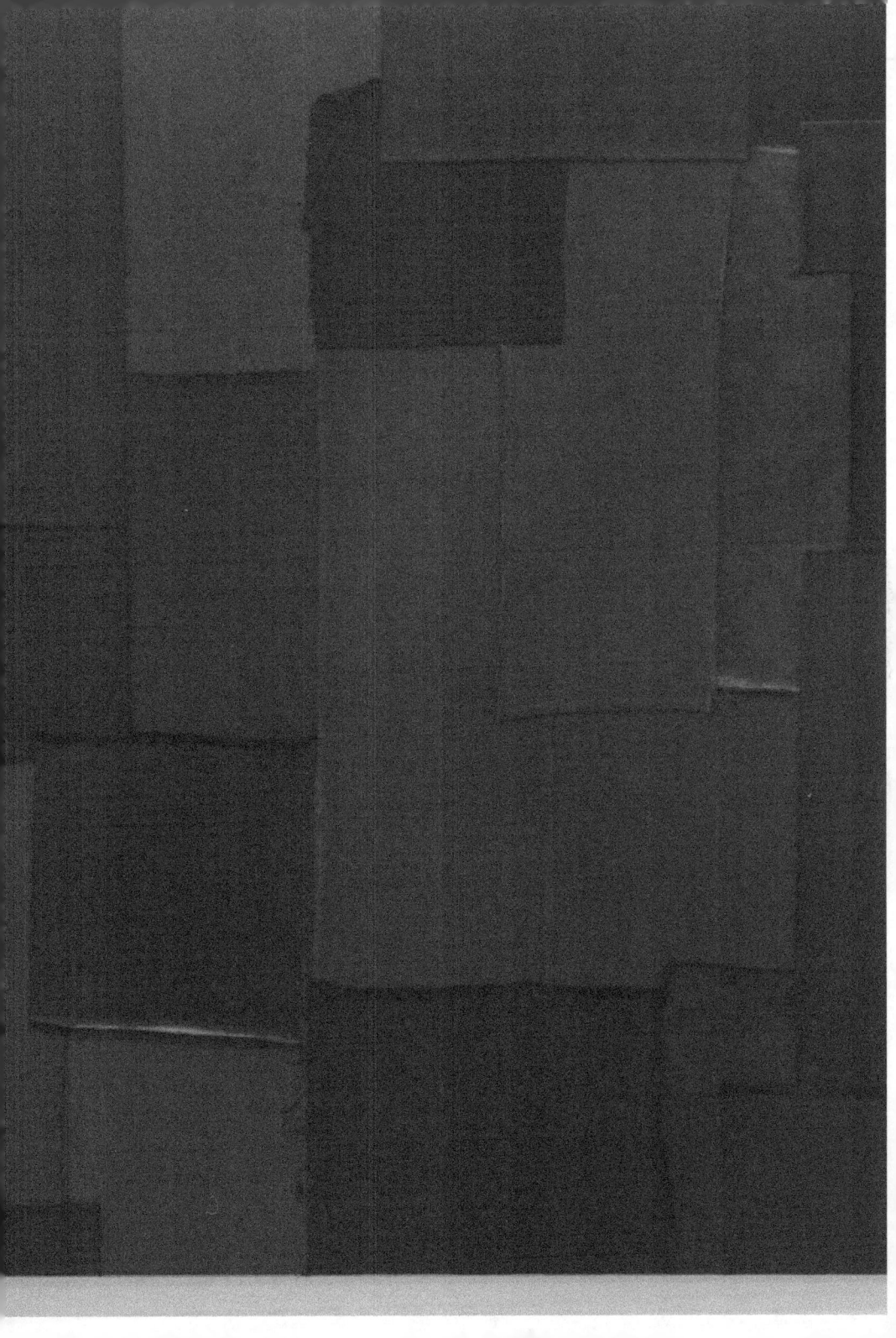

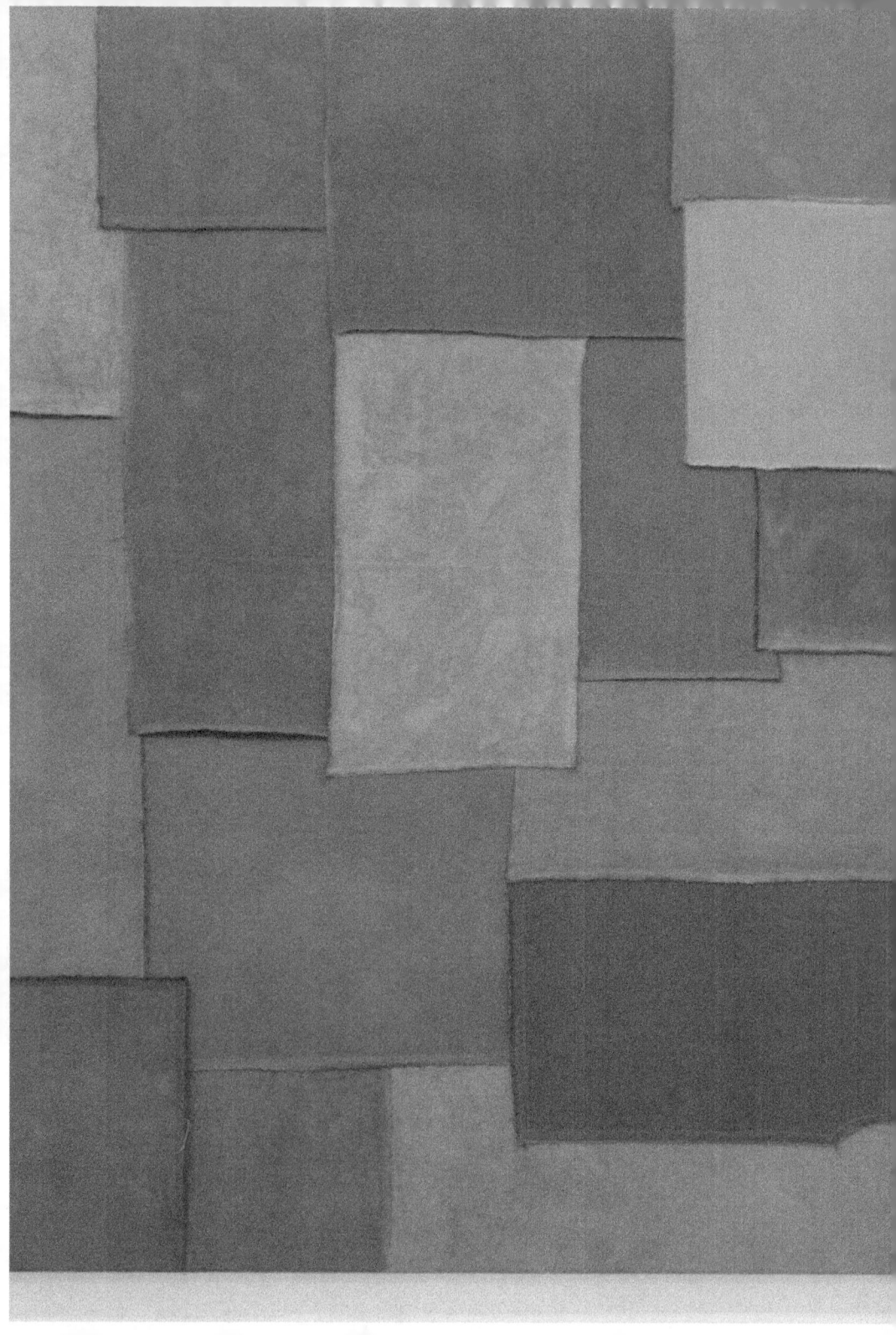

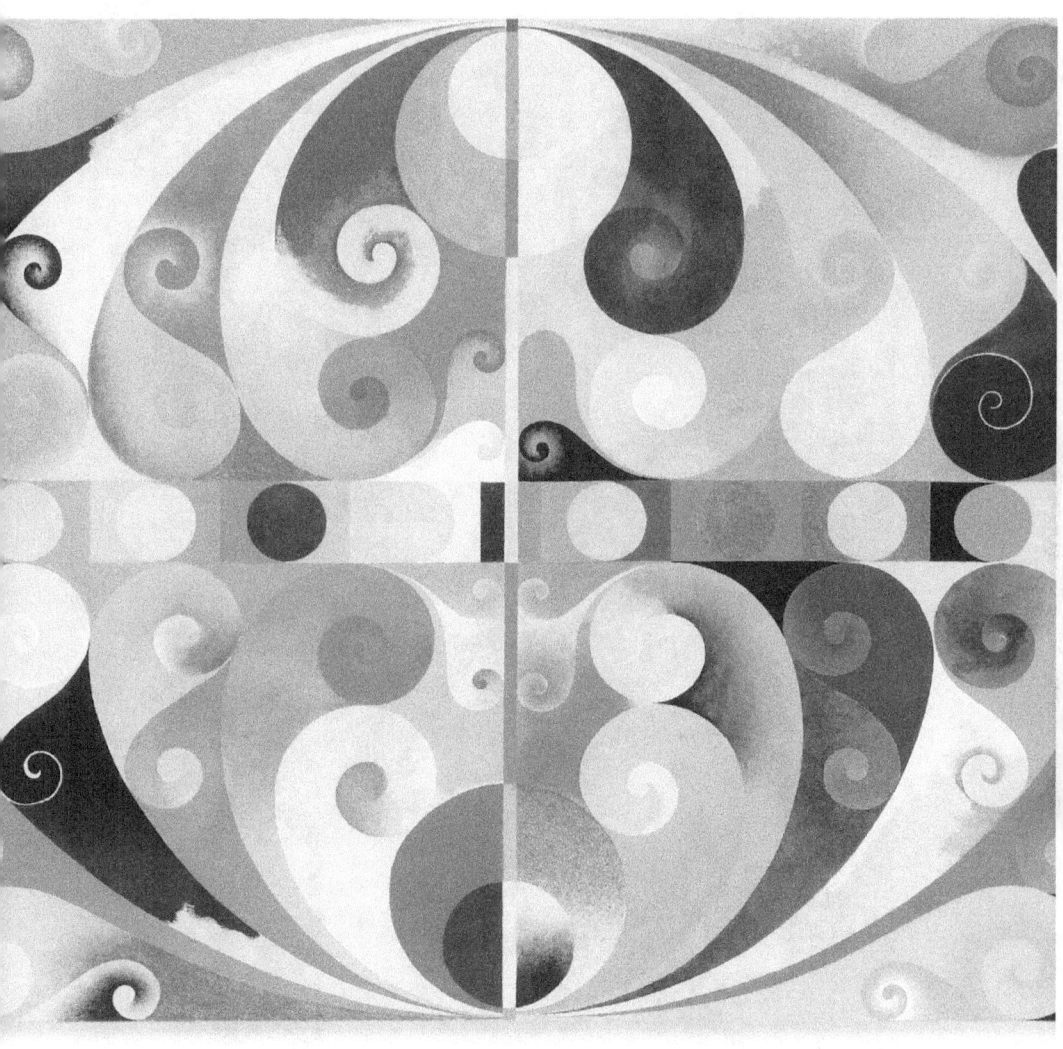

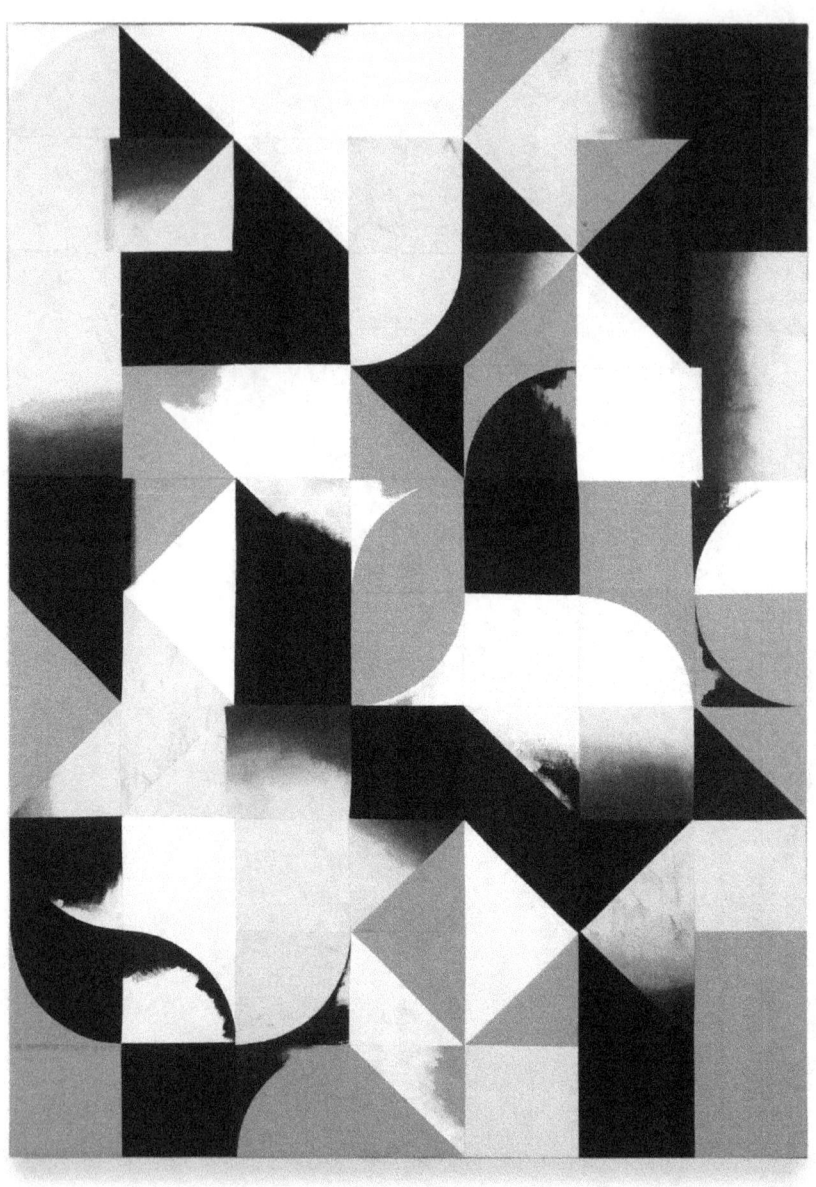

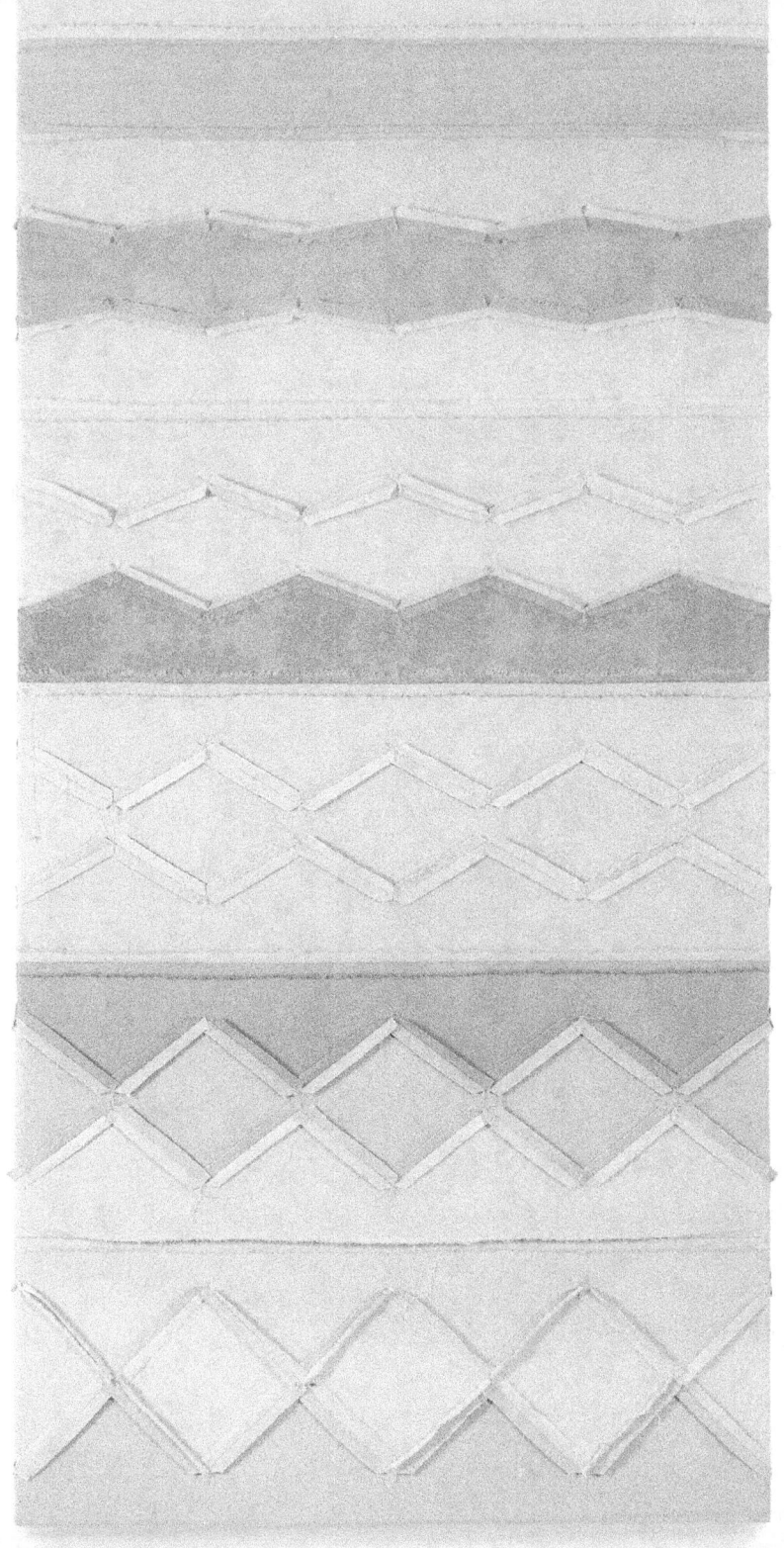

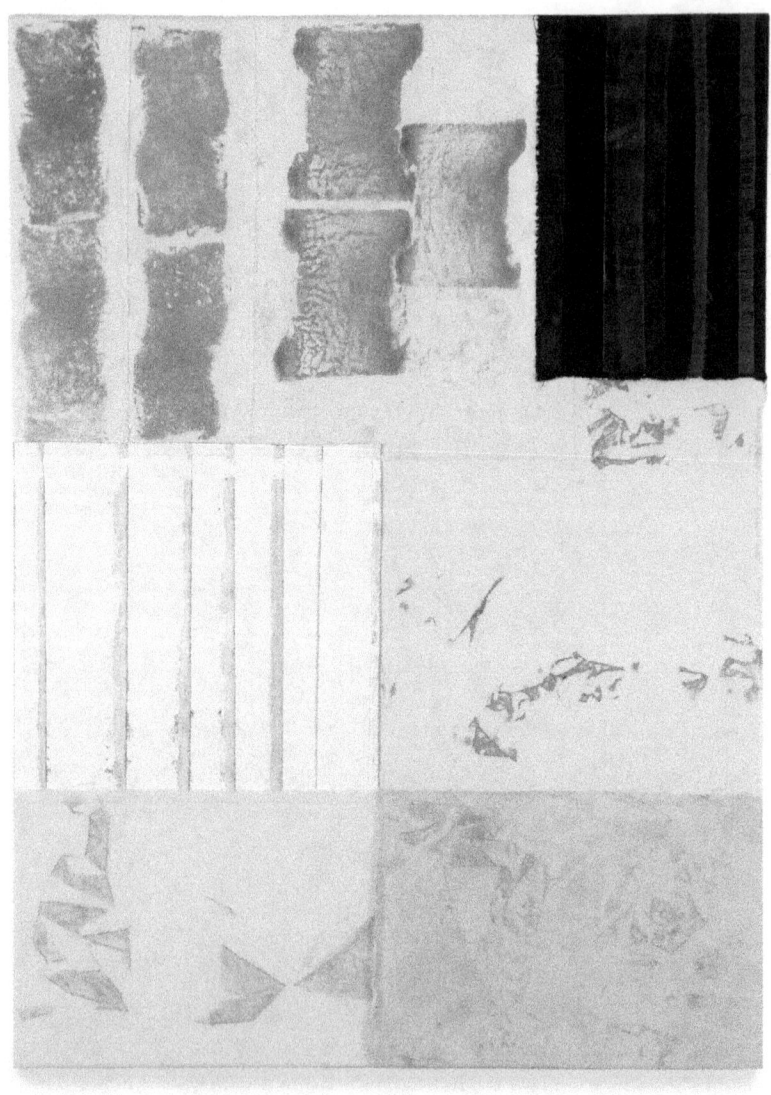

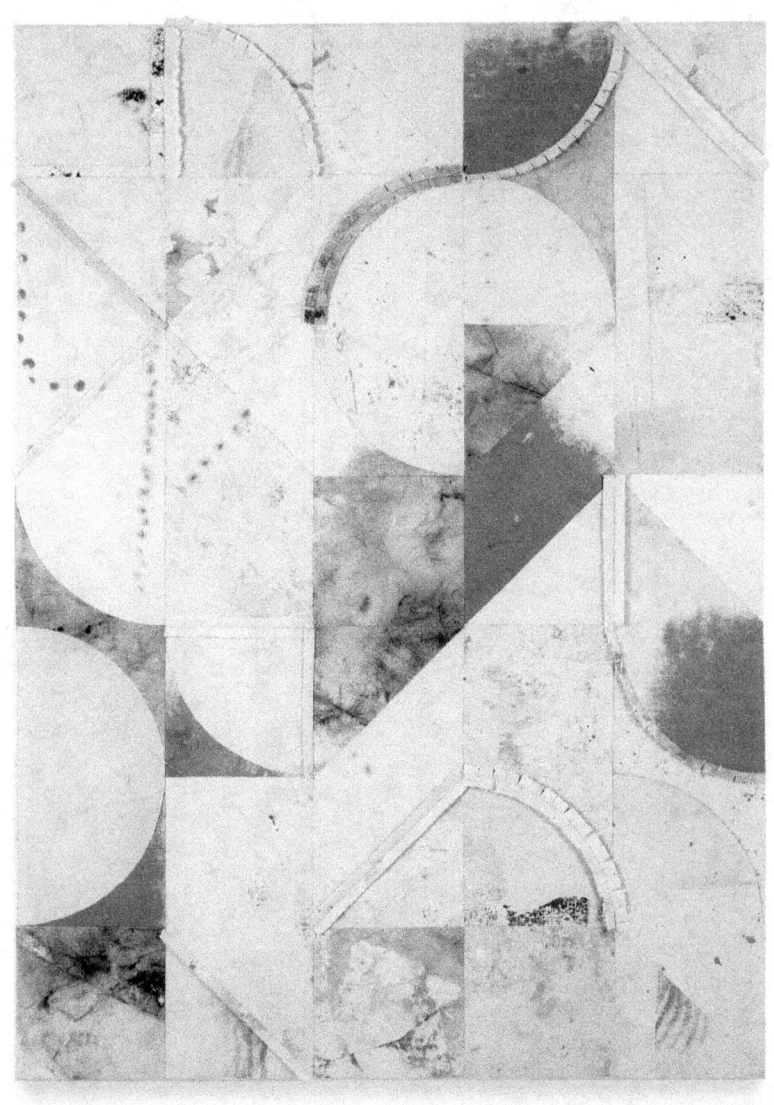

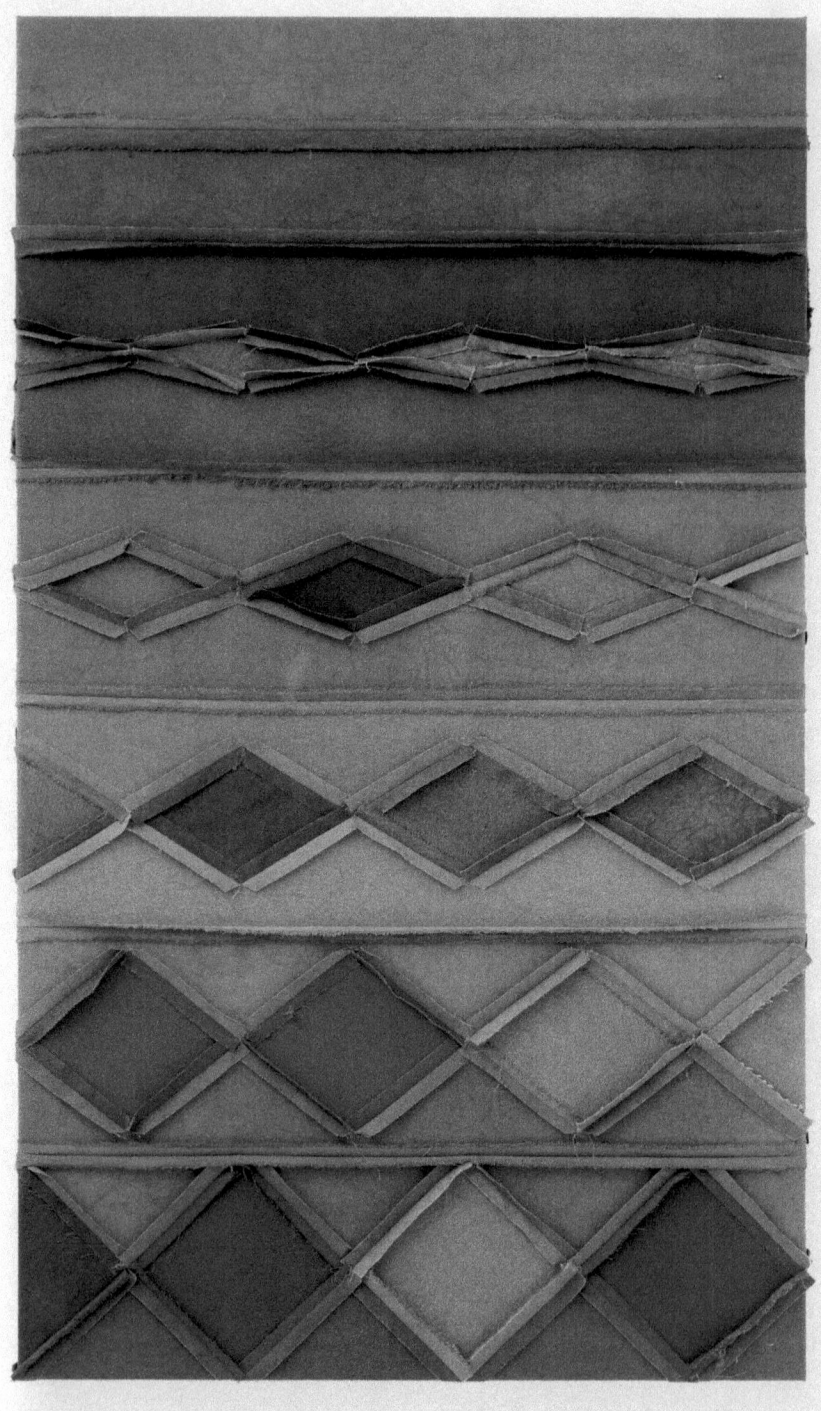

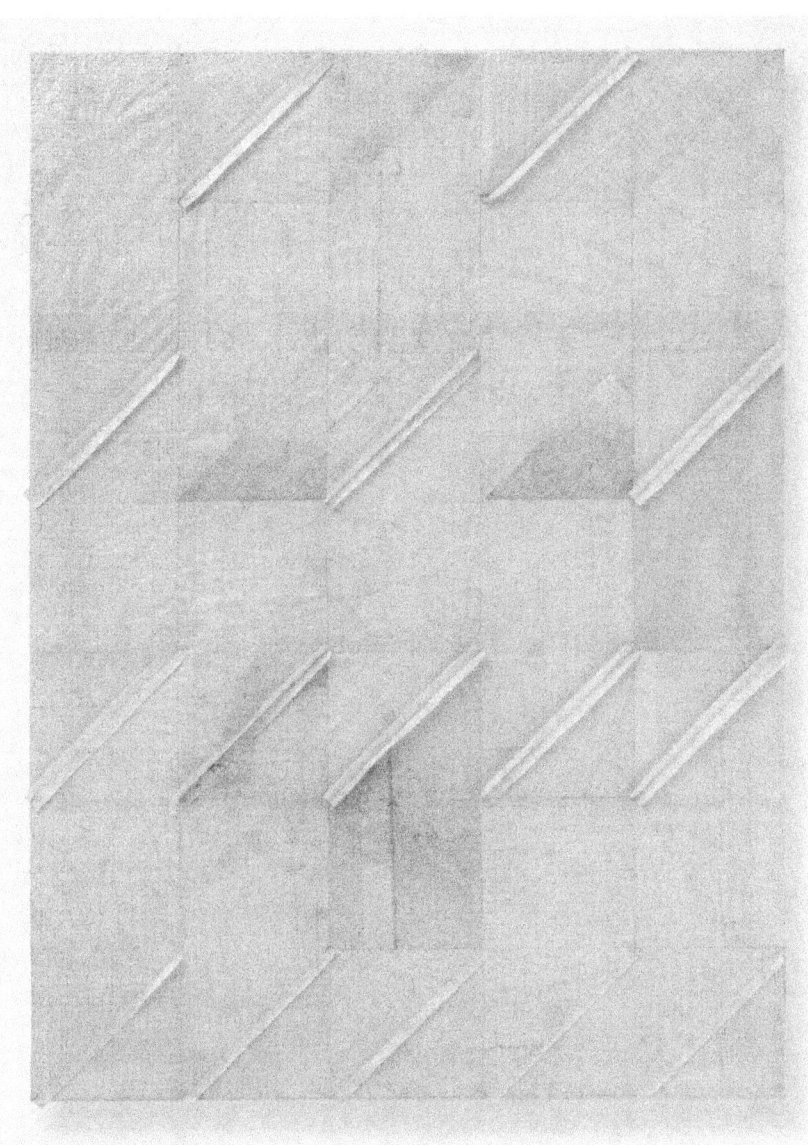

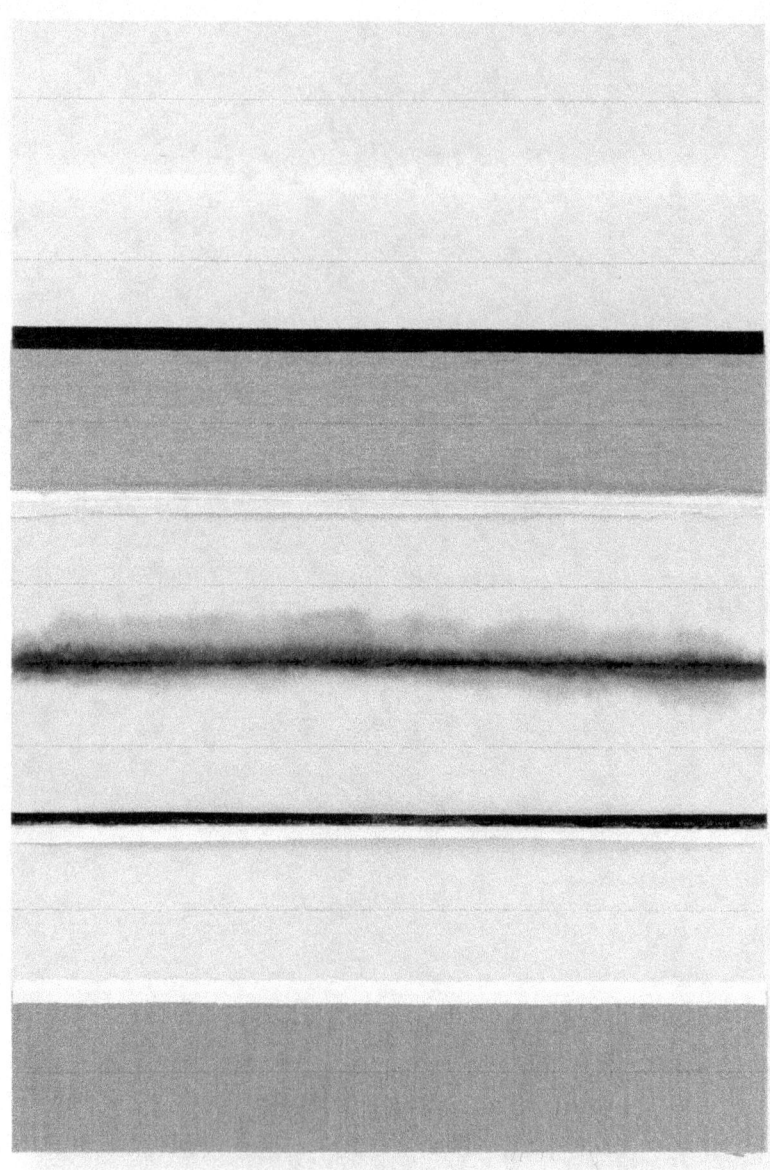

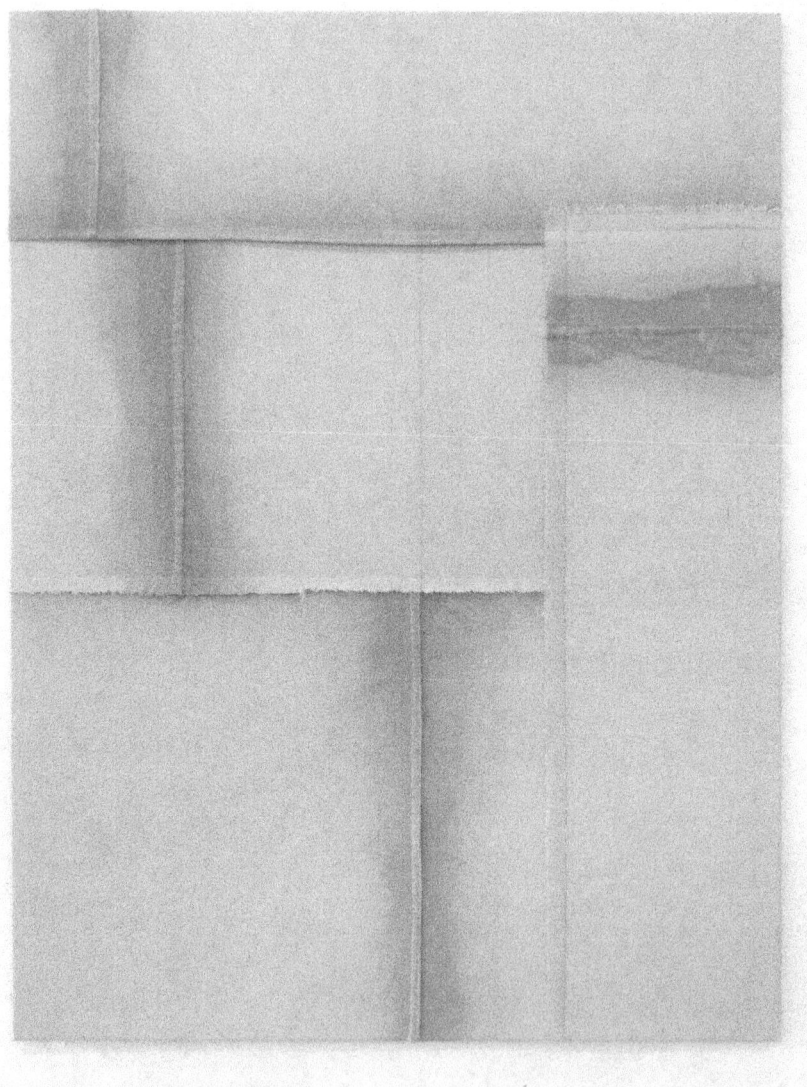

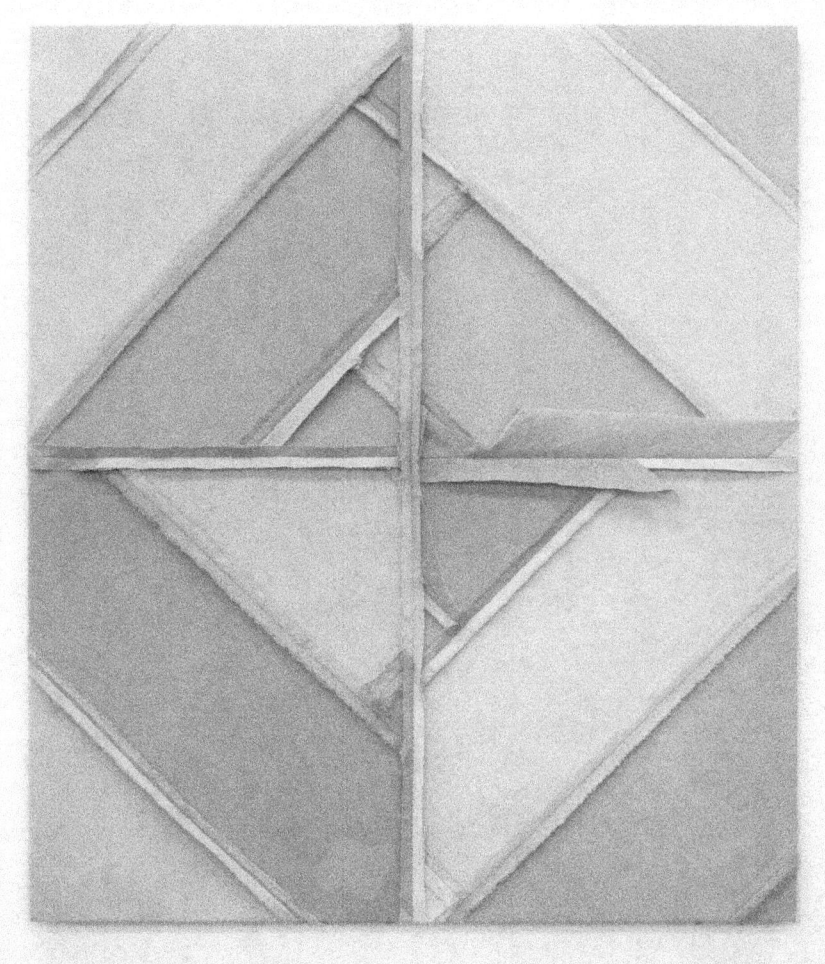

119

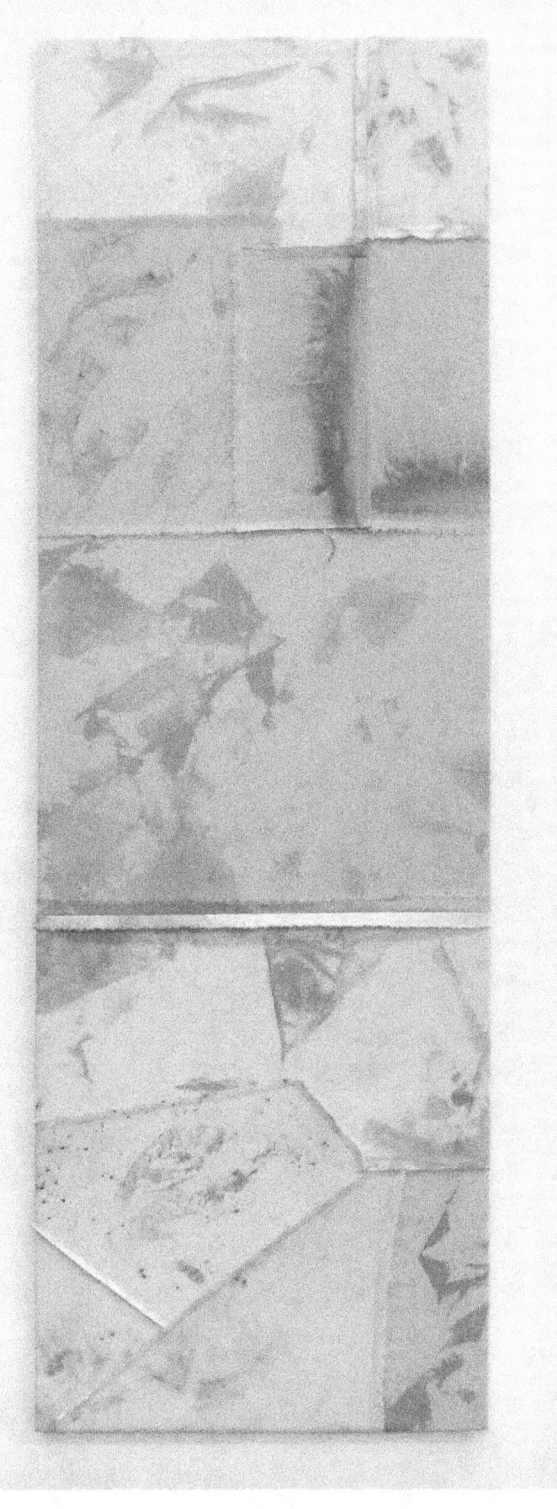

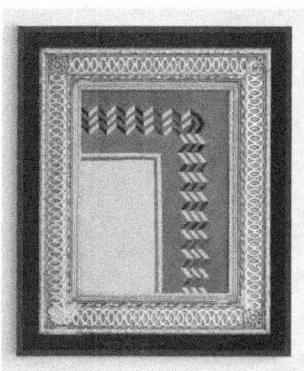

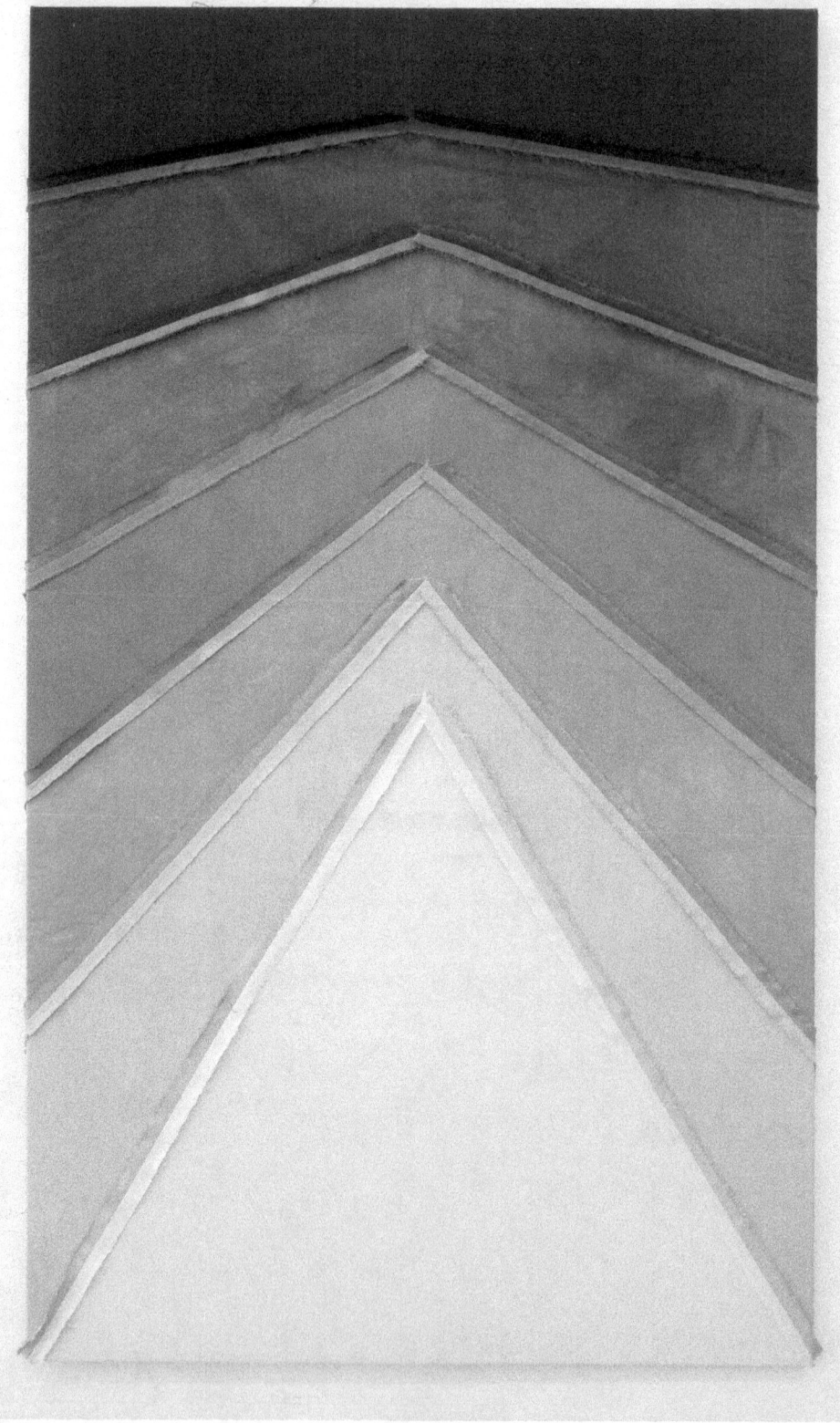

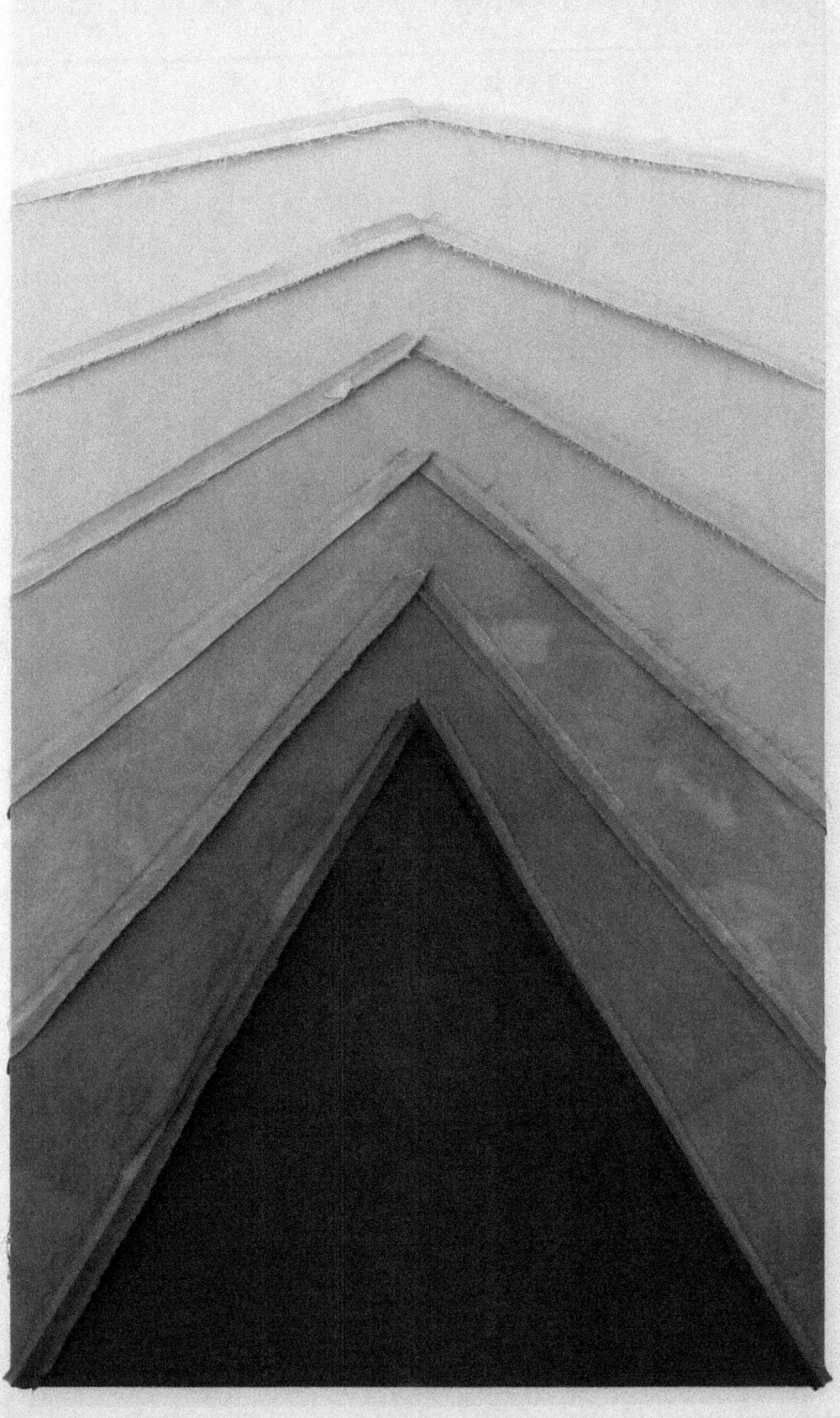

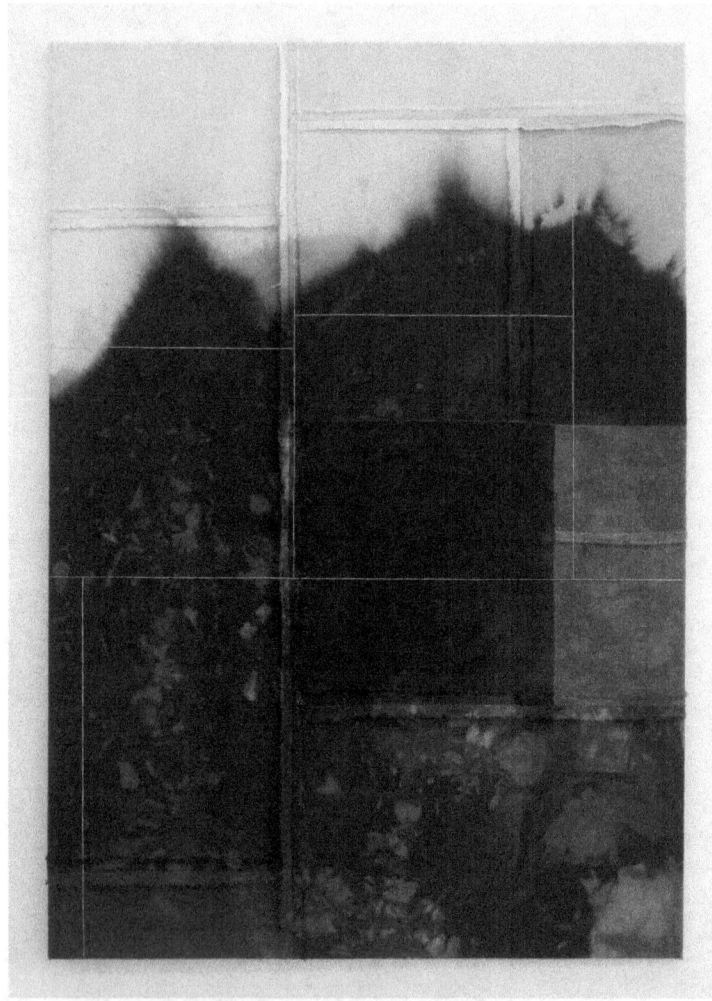

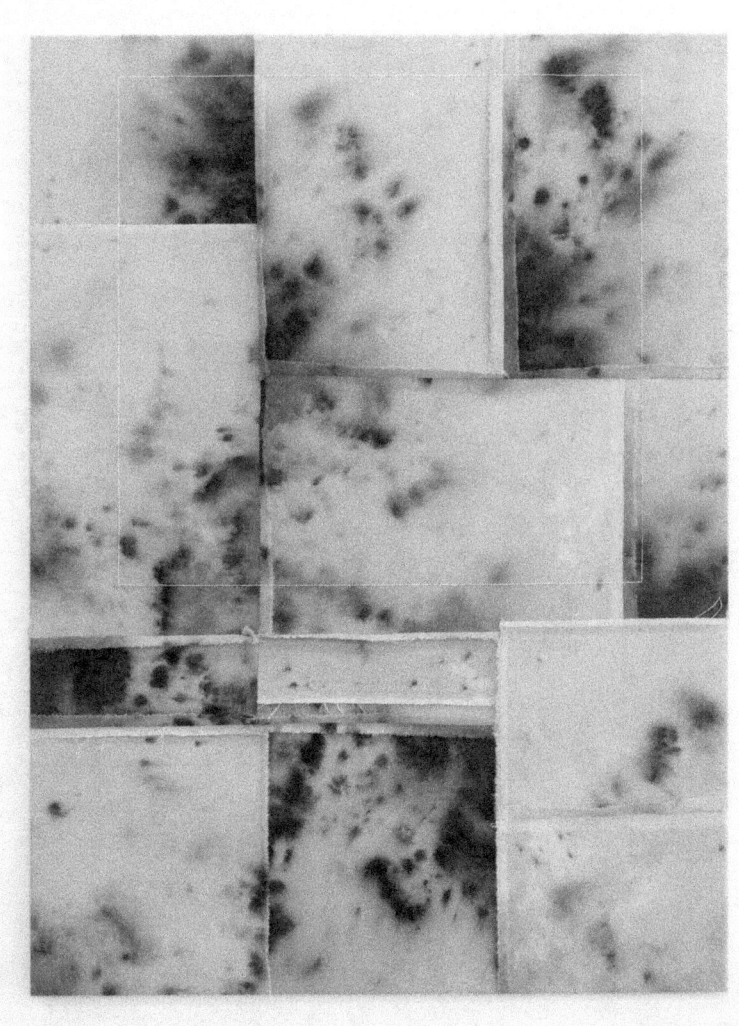

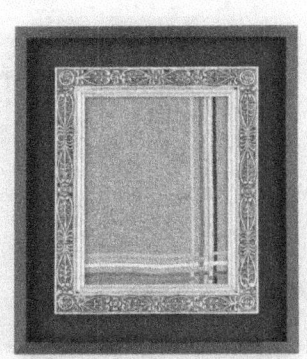

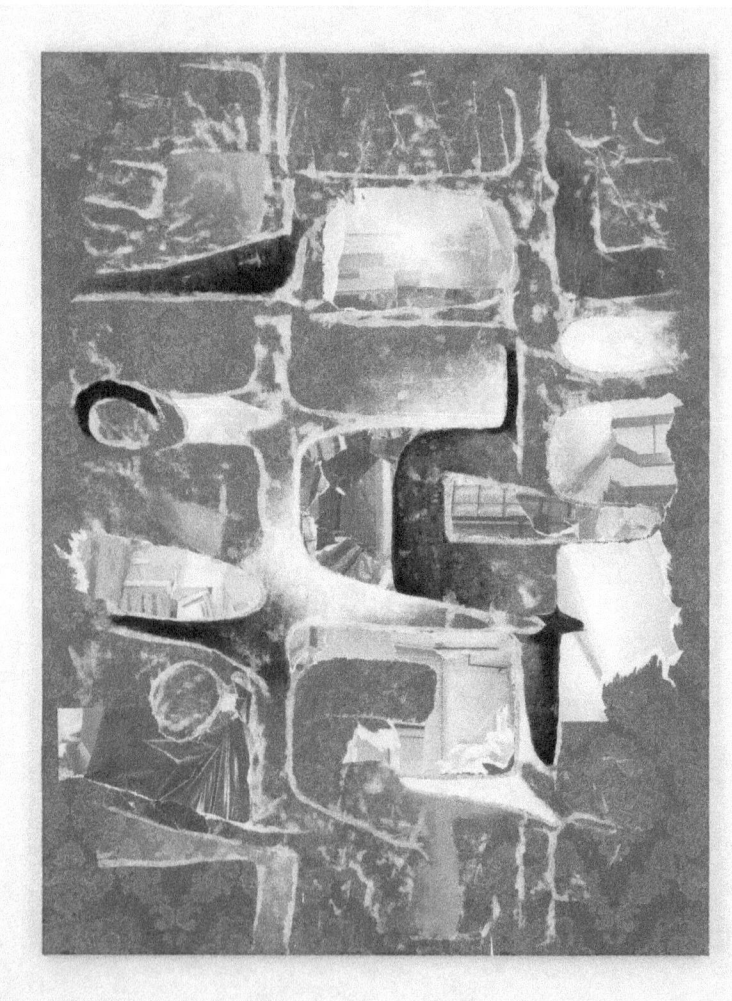

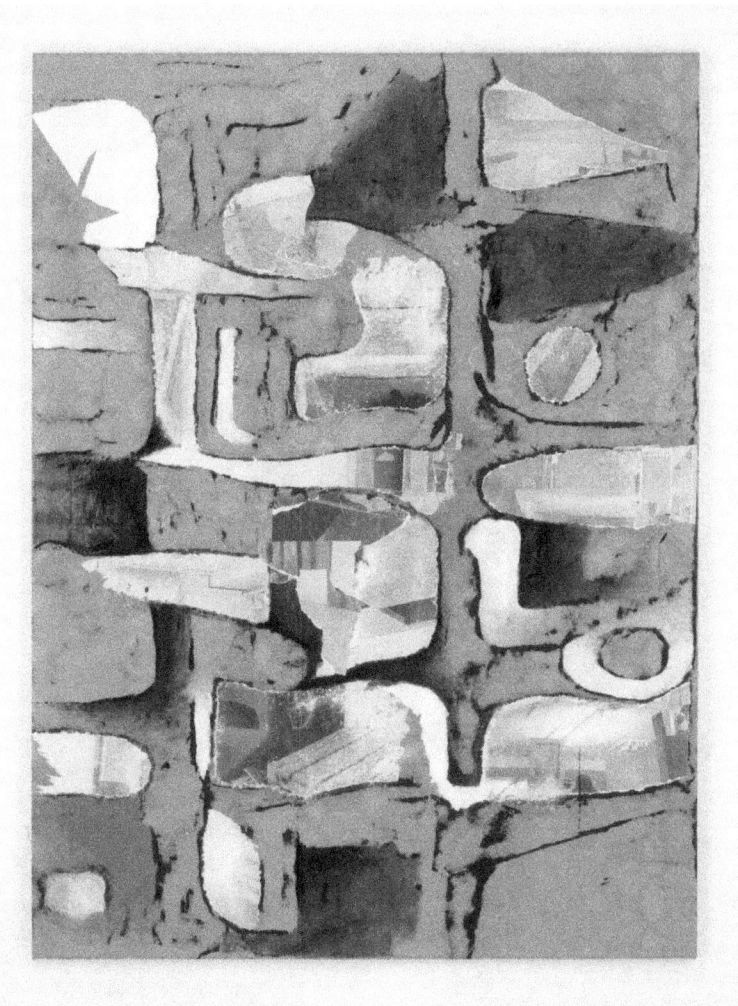

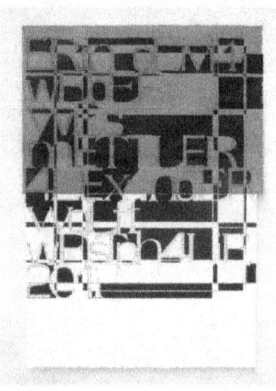

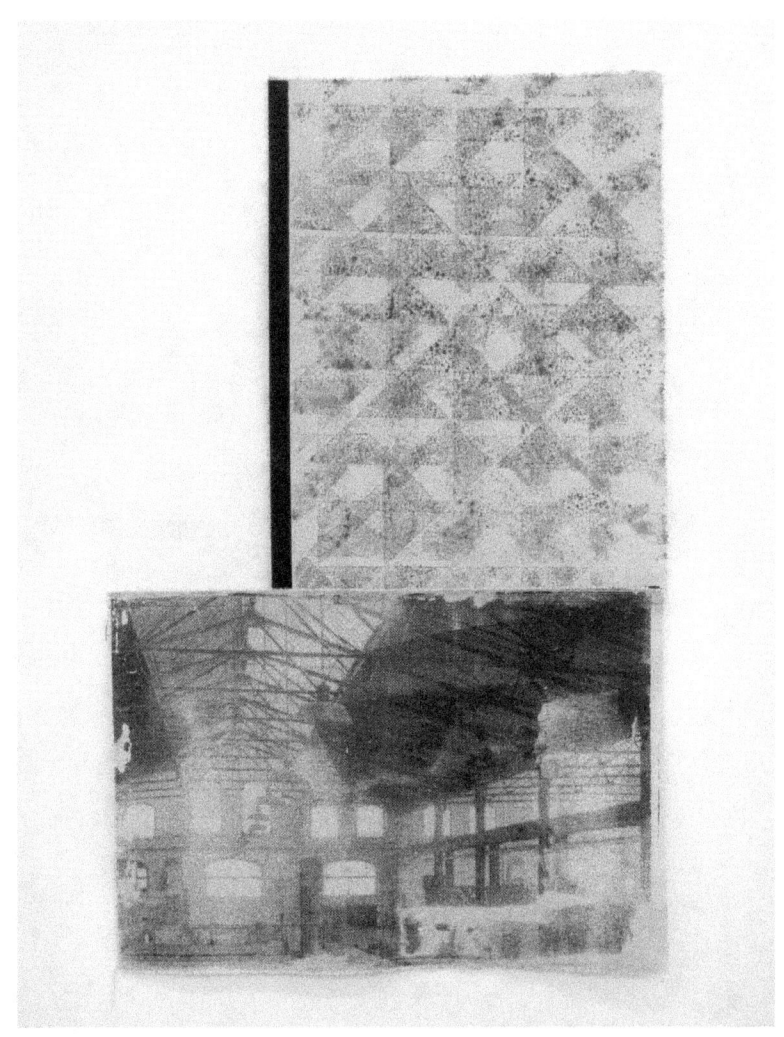

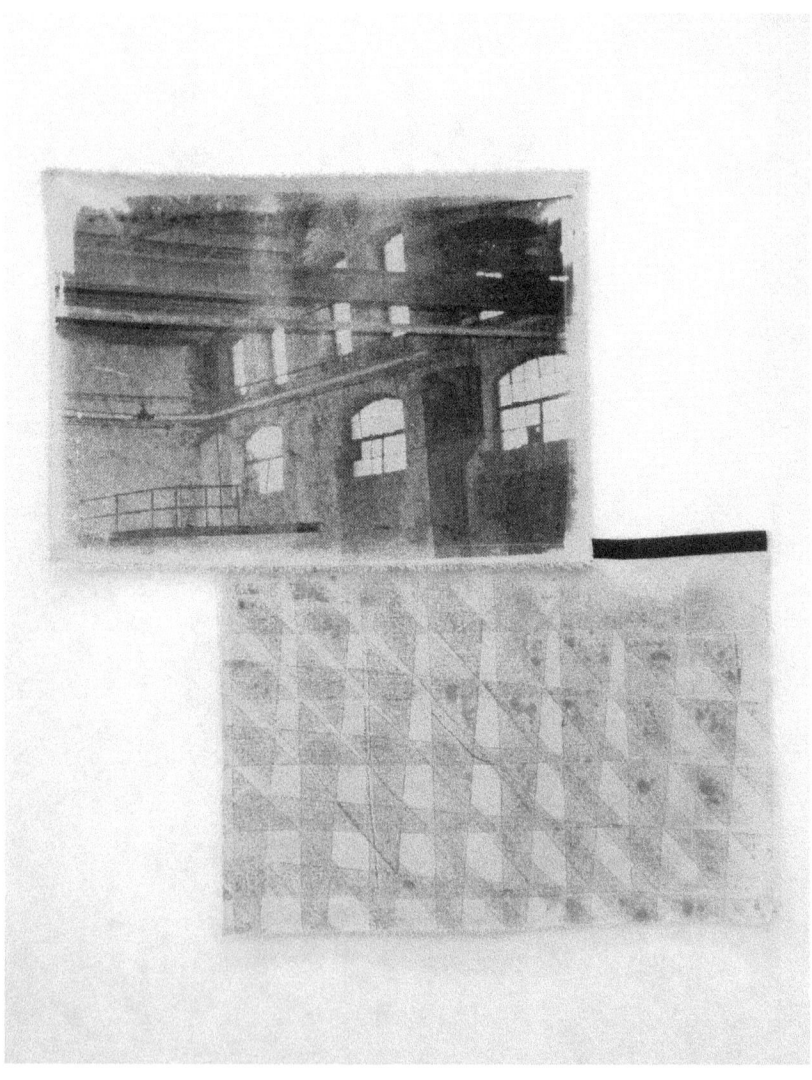

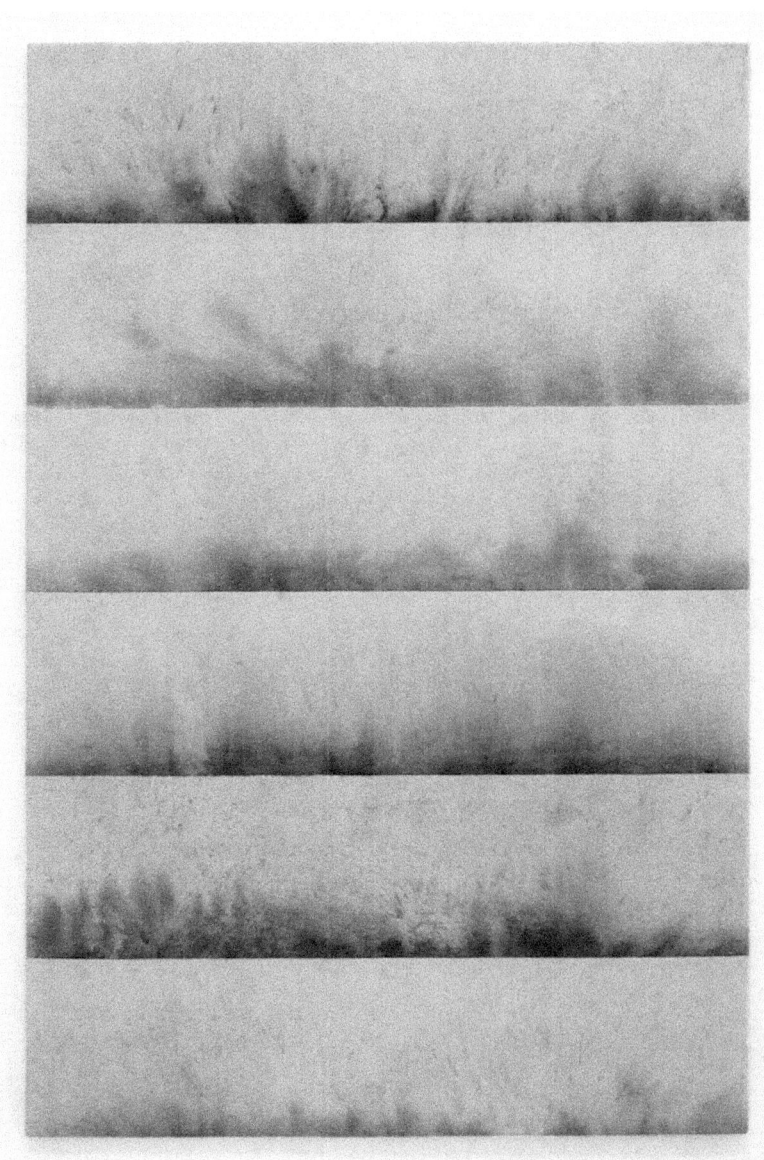

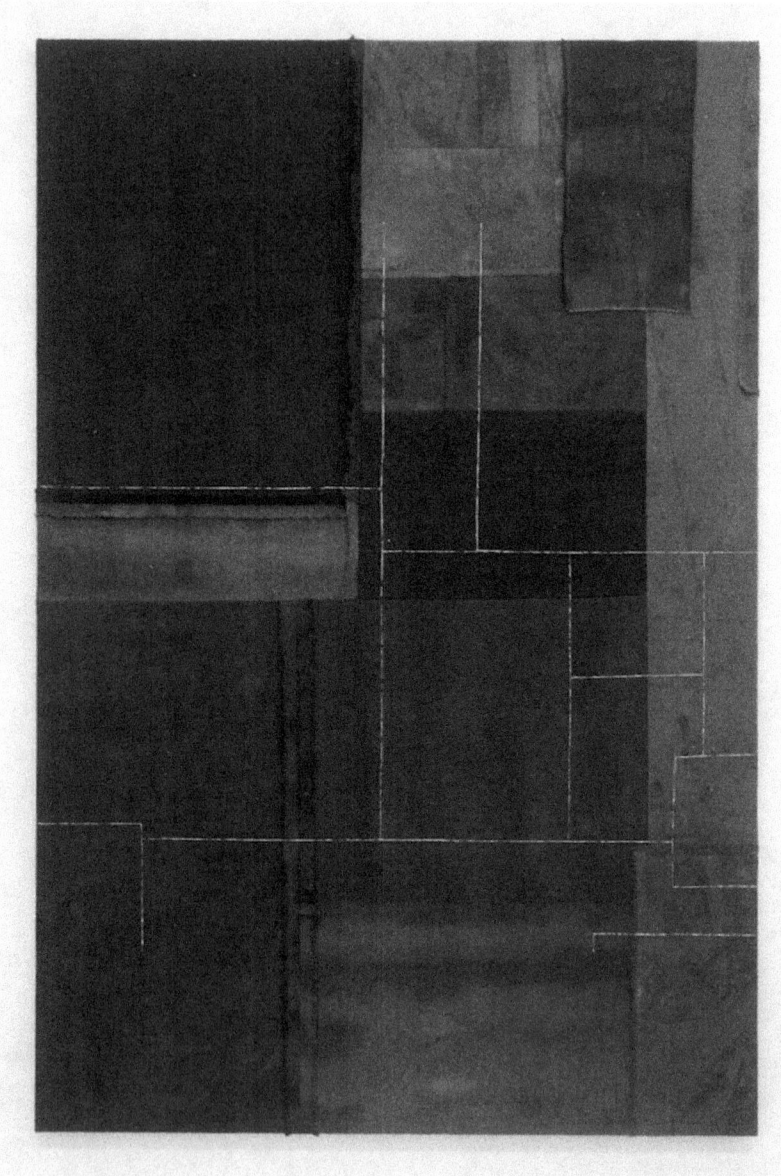

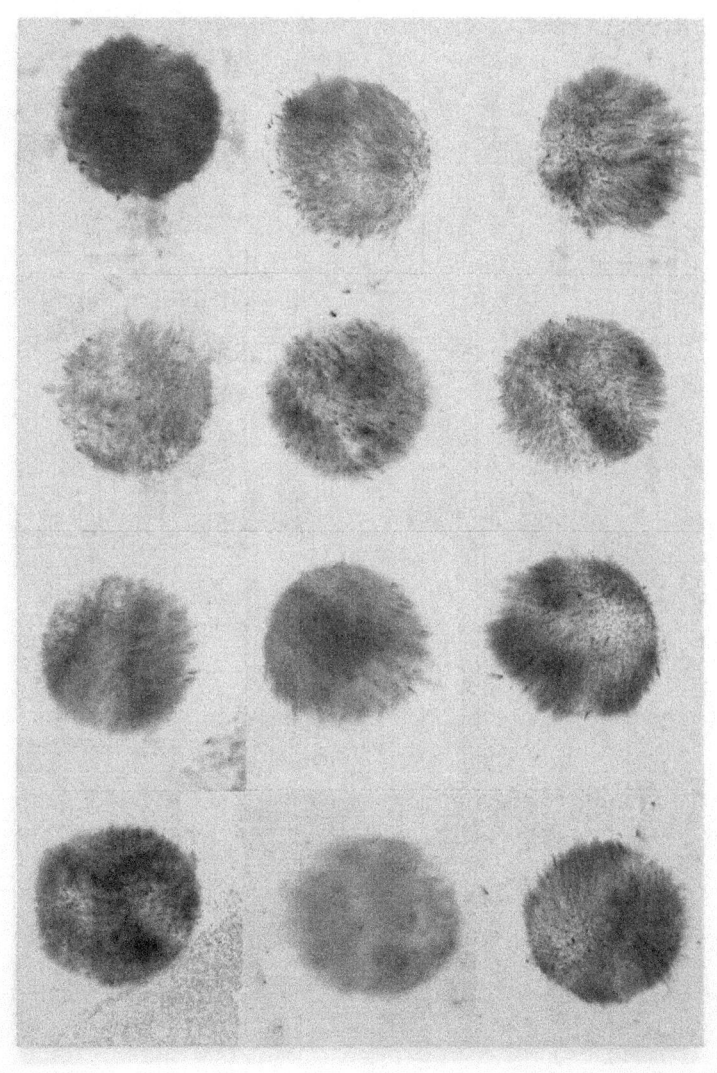

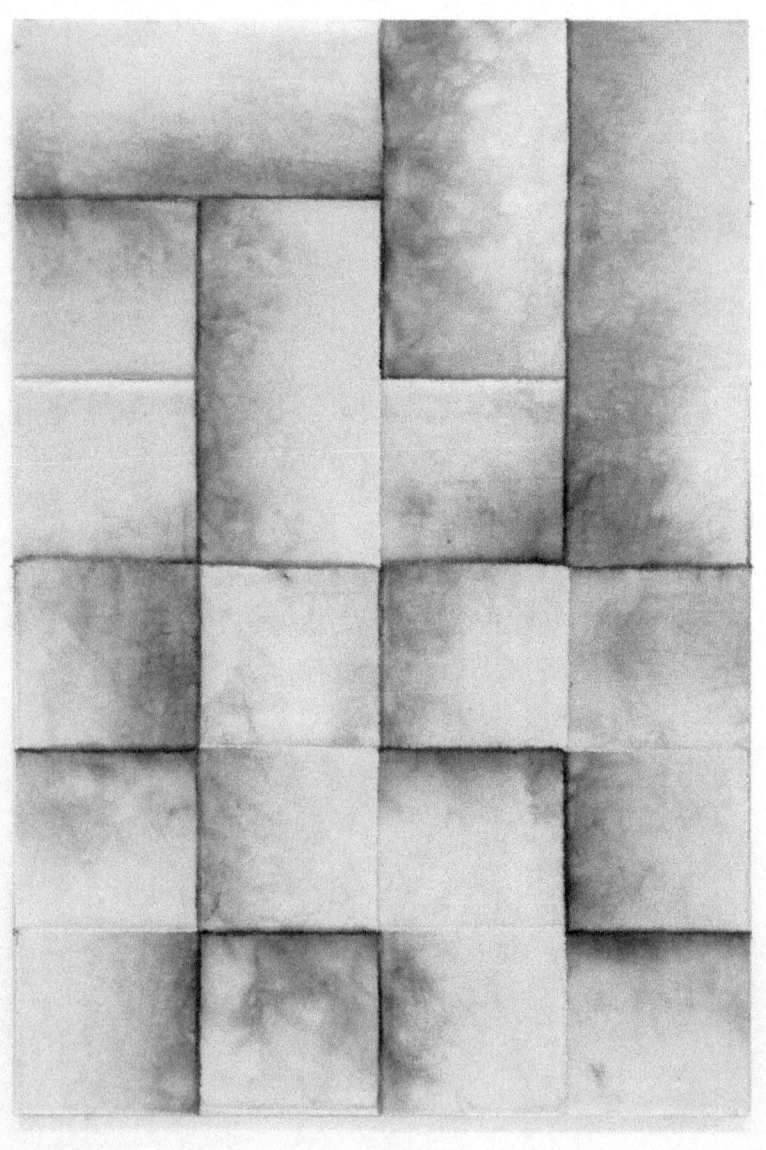

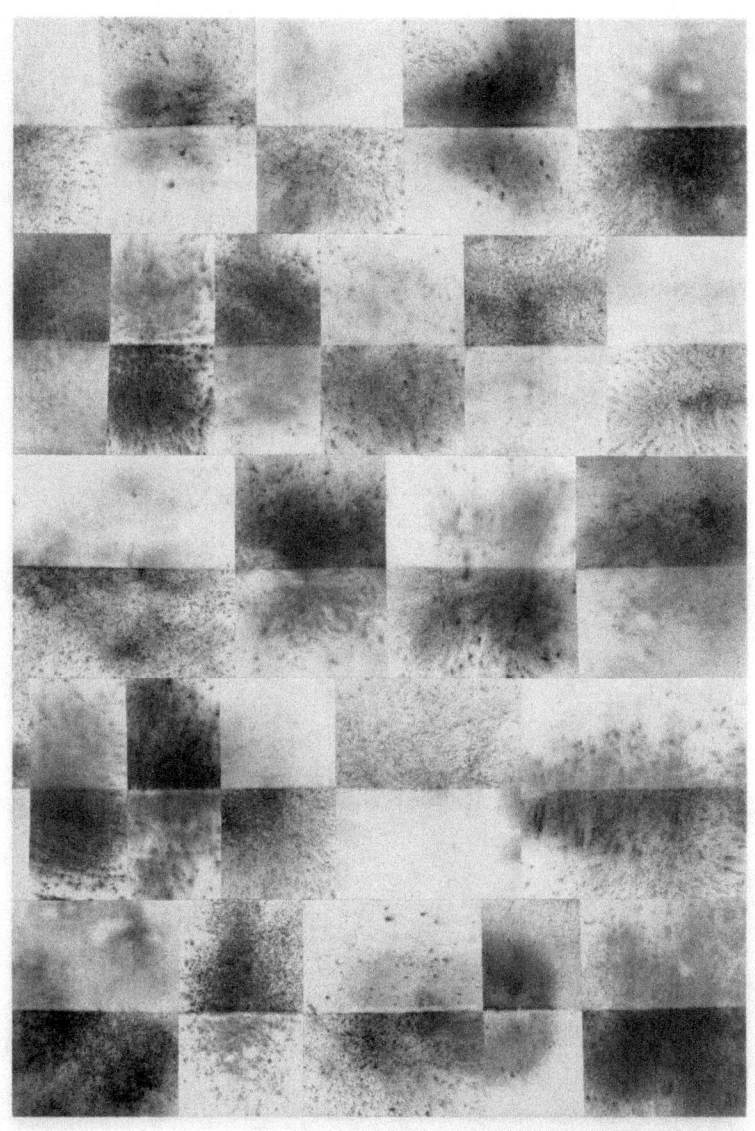

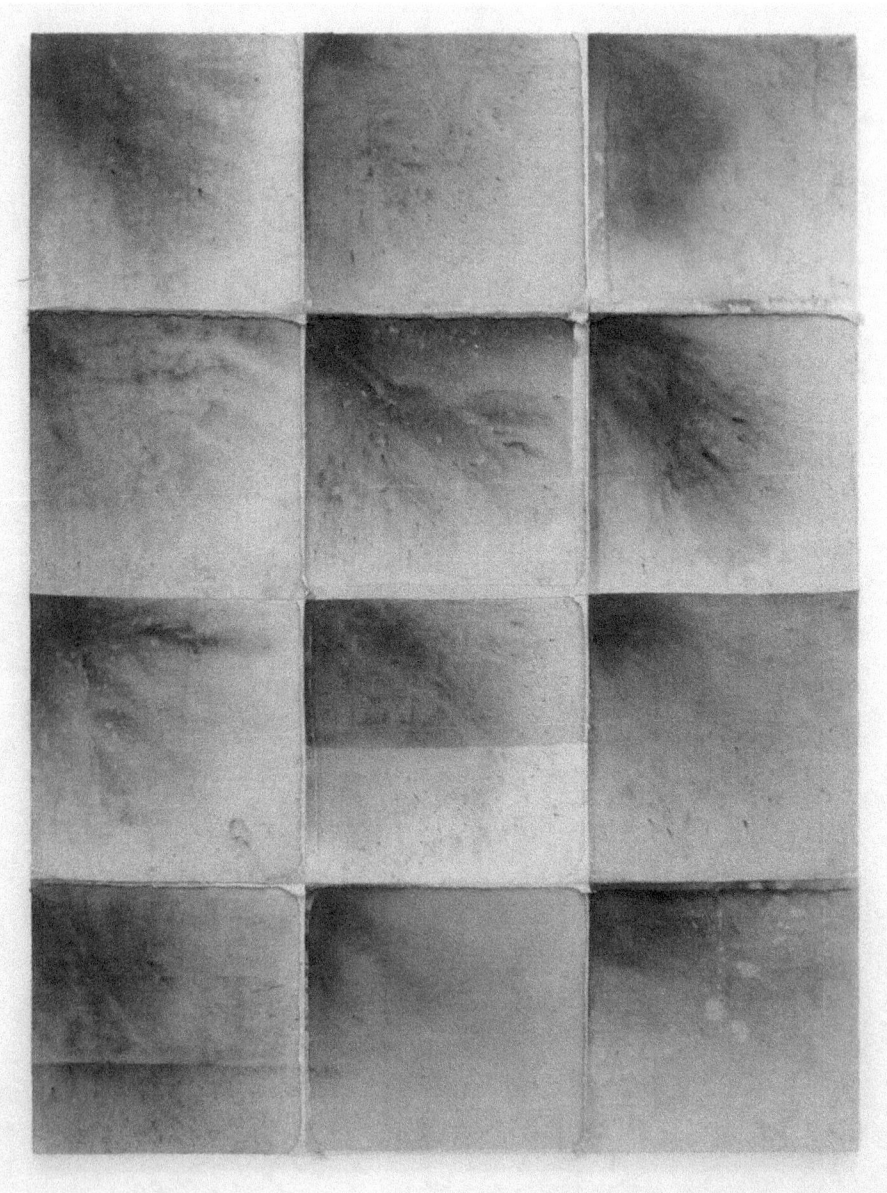

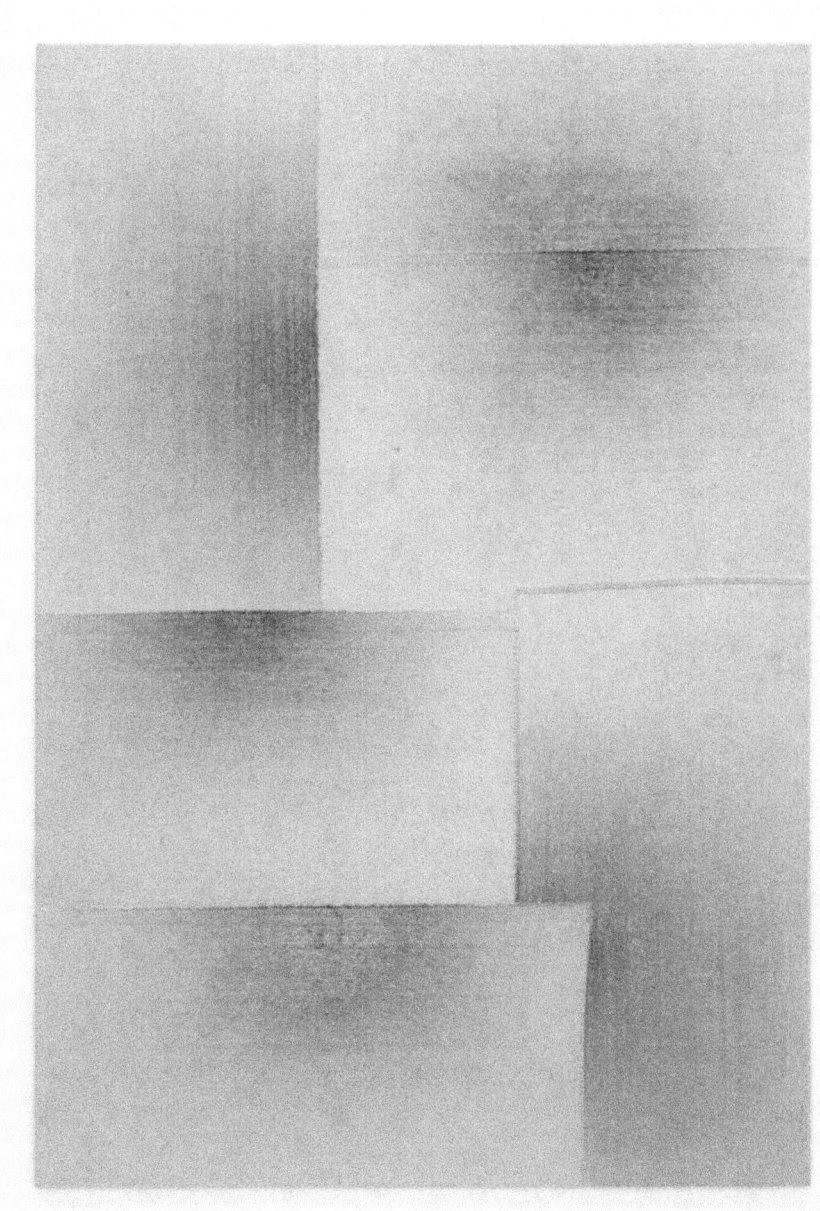

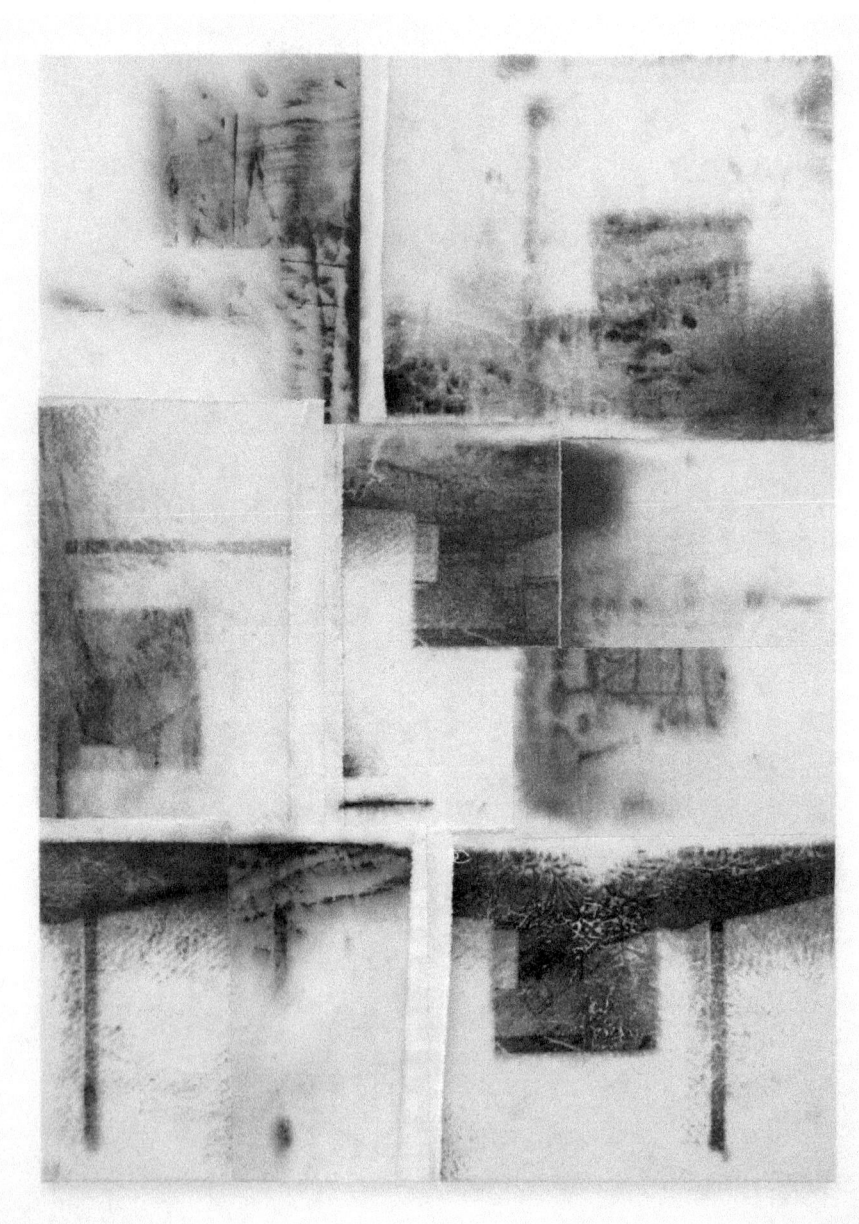

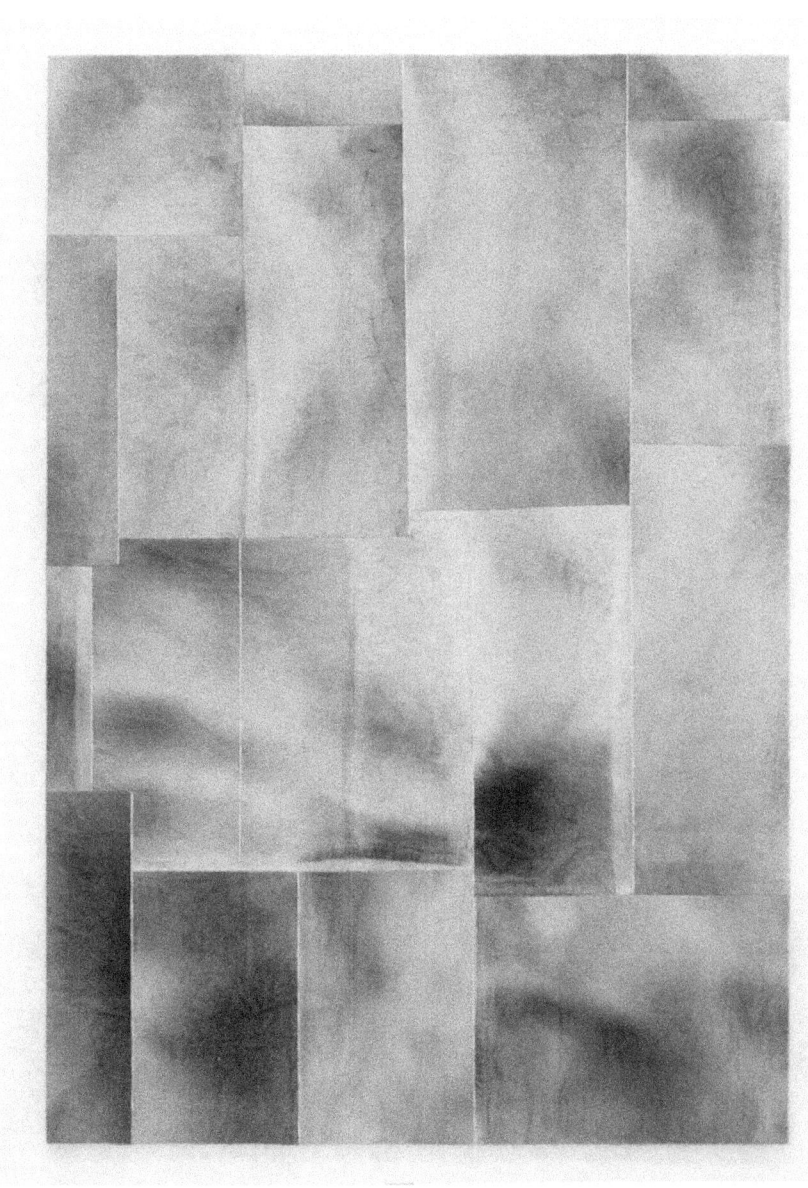

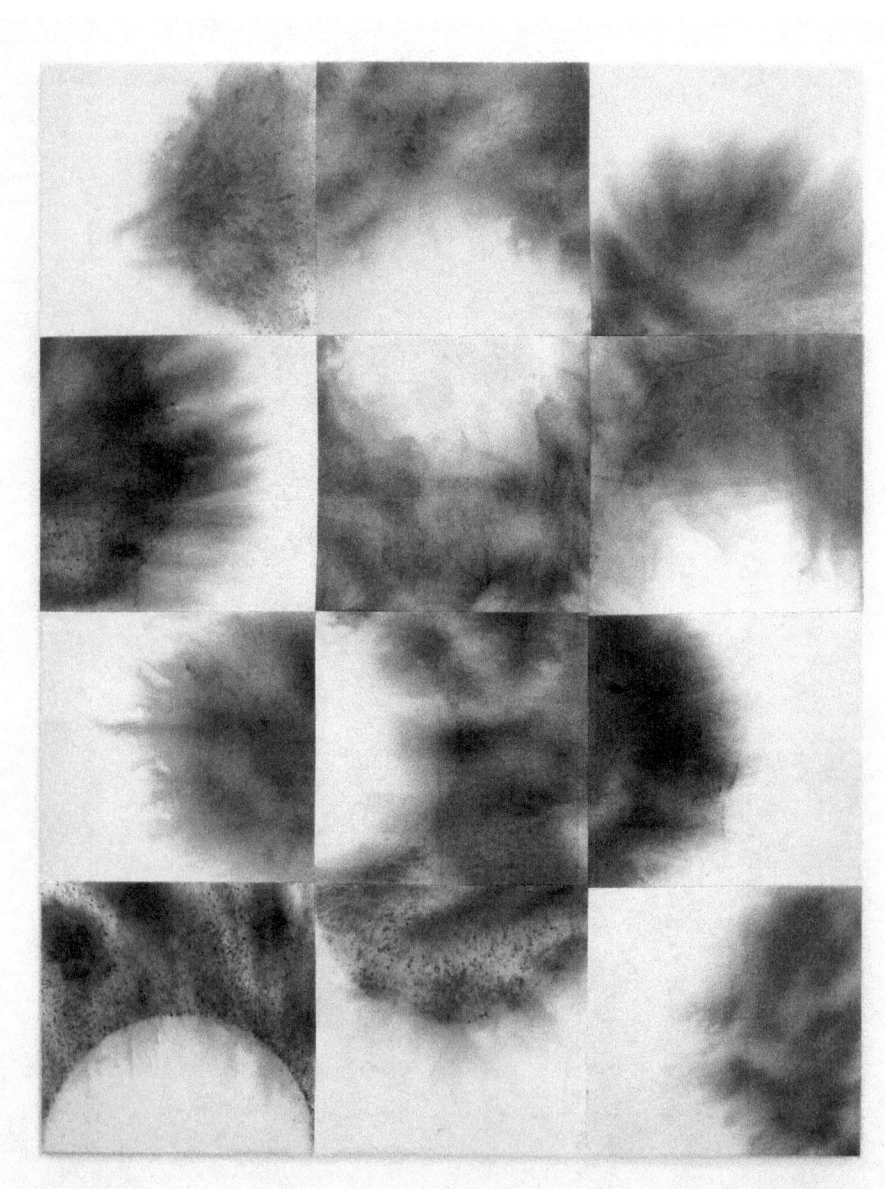

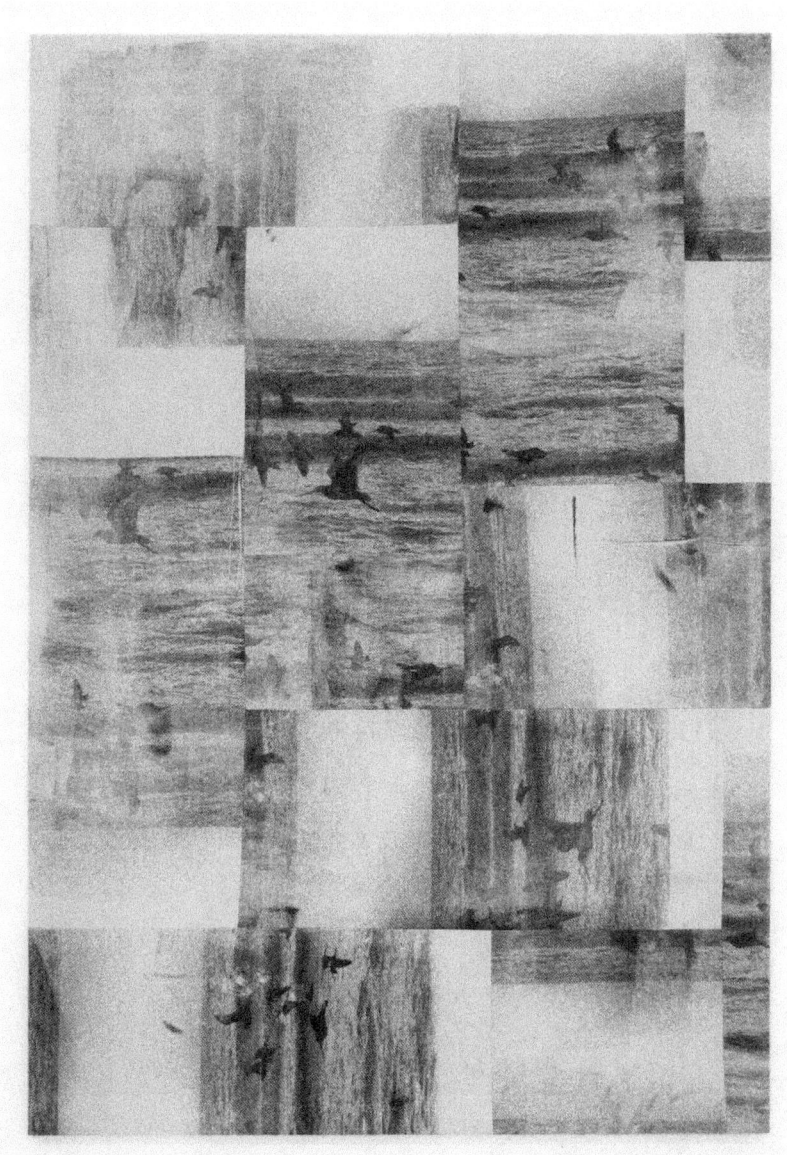

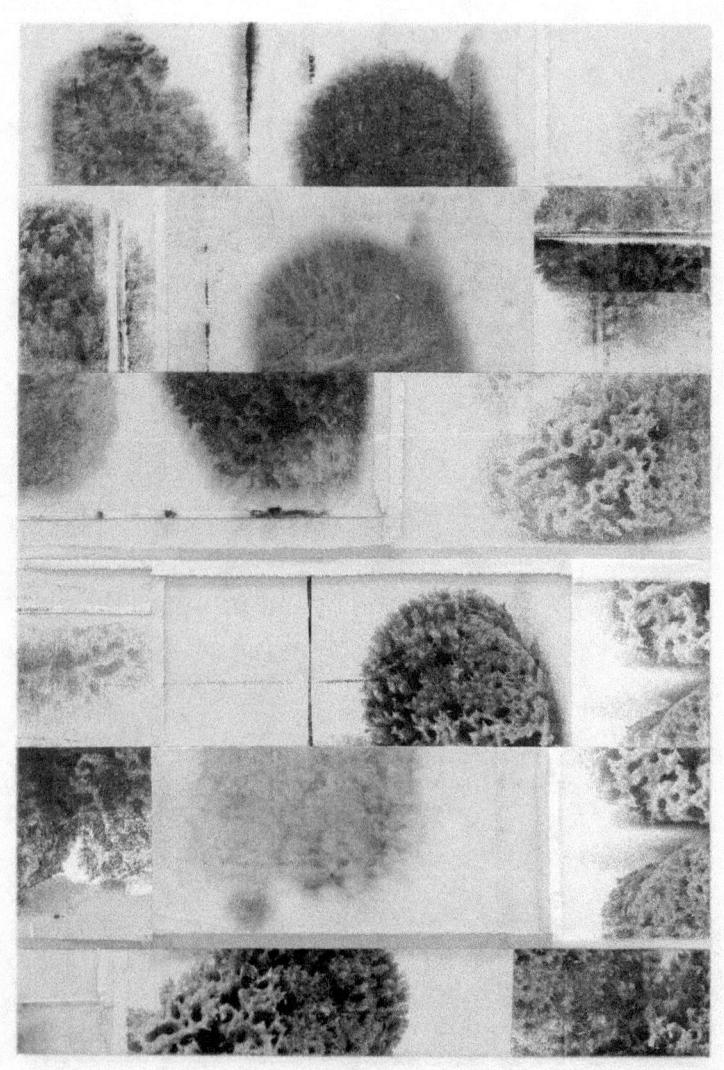

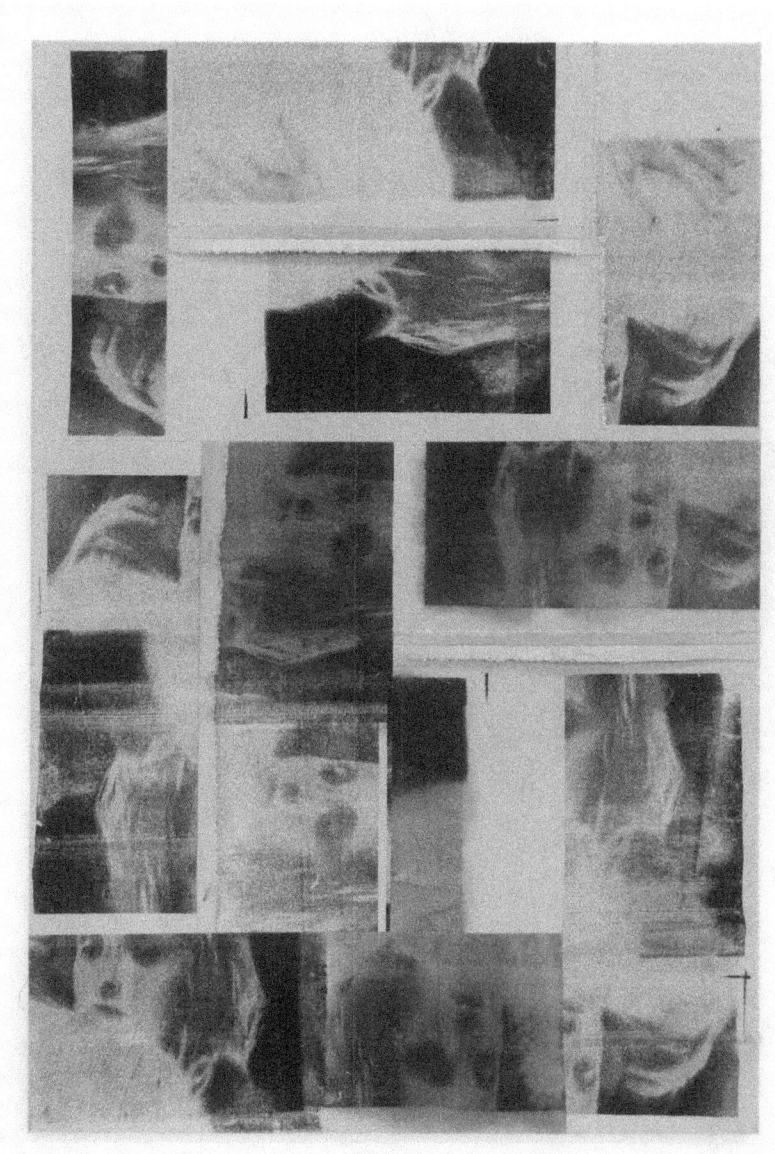

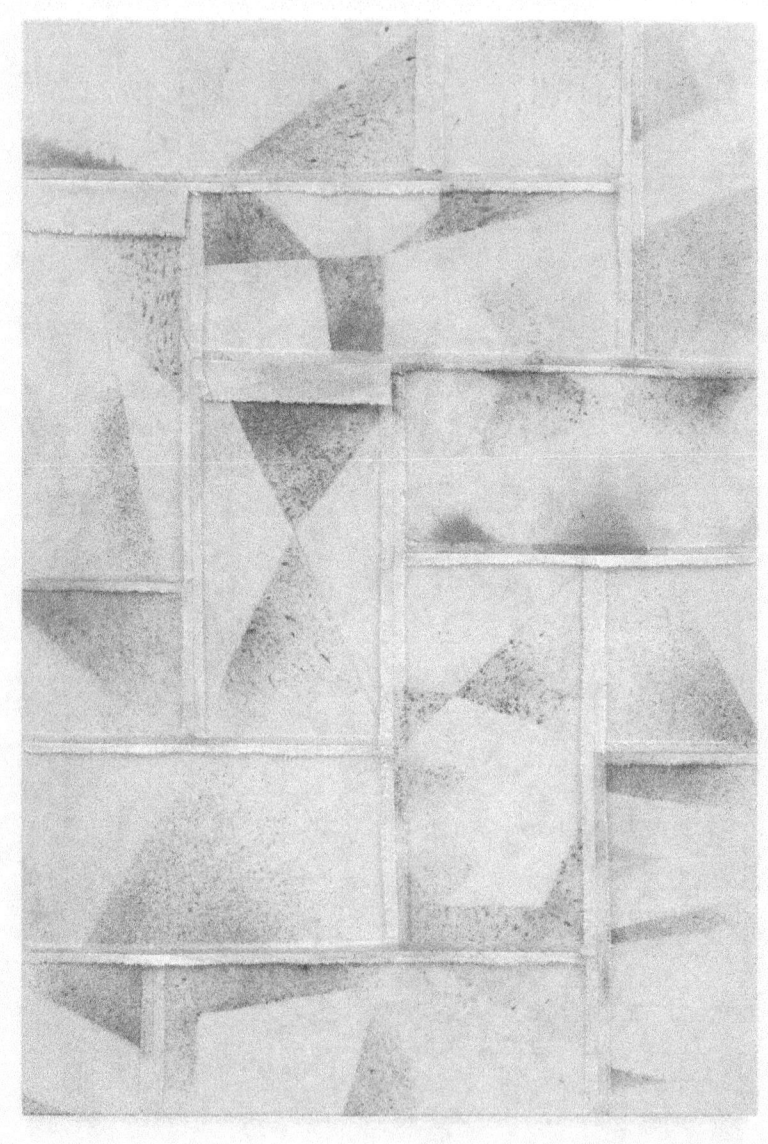

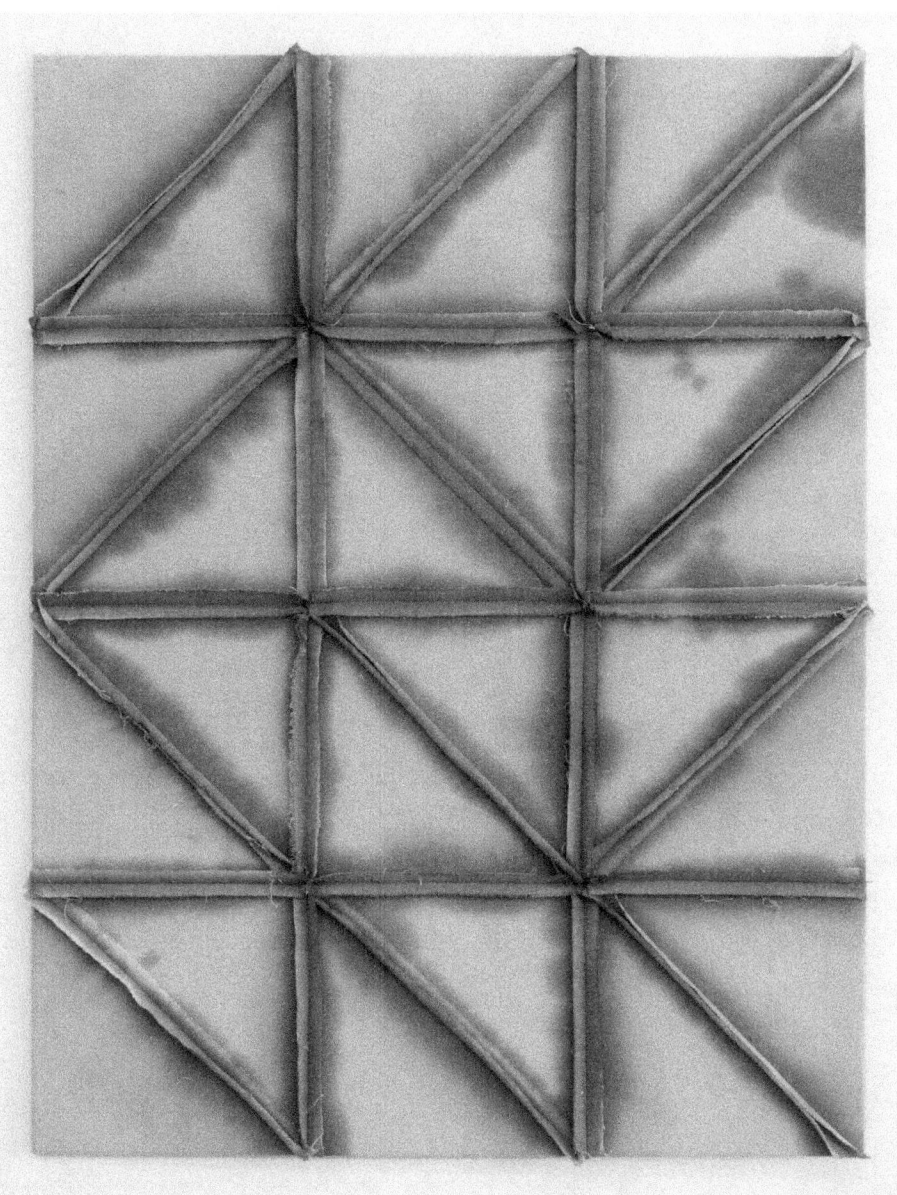

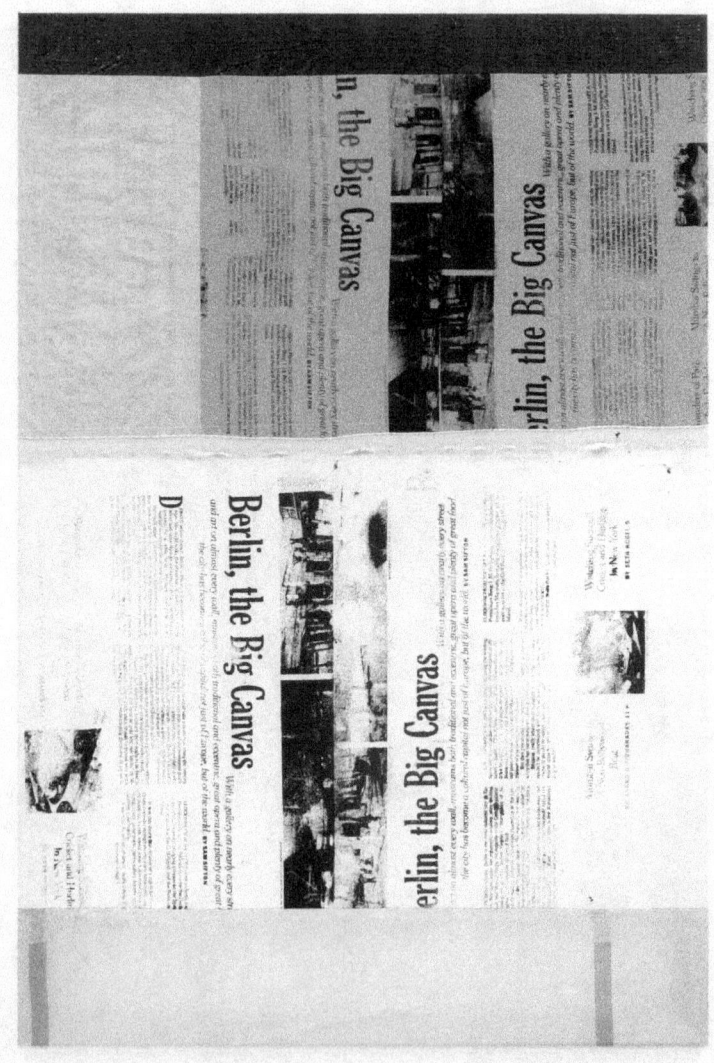

Berlin, the Big Canvas

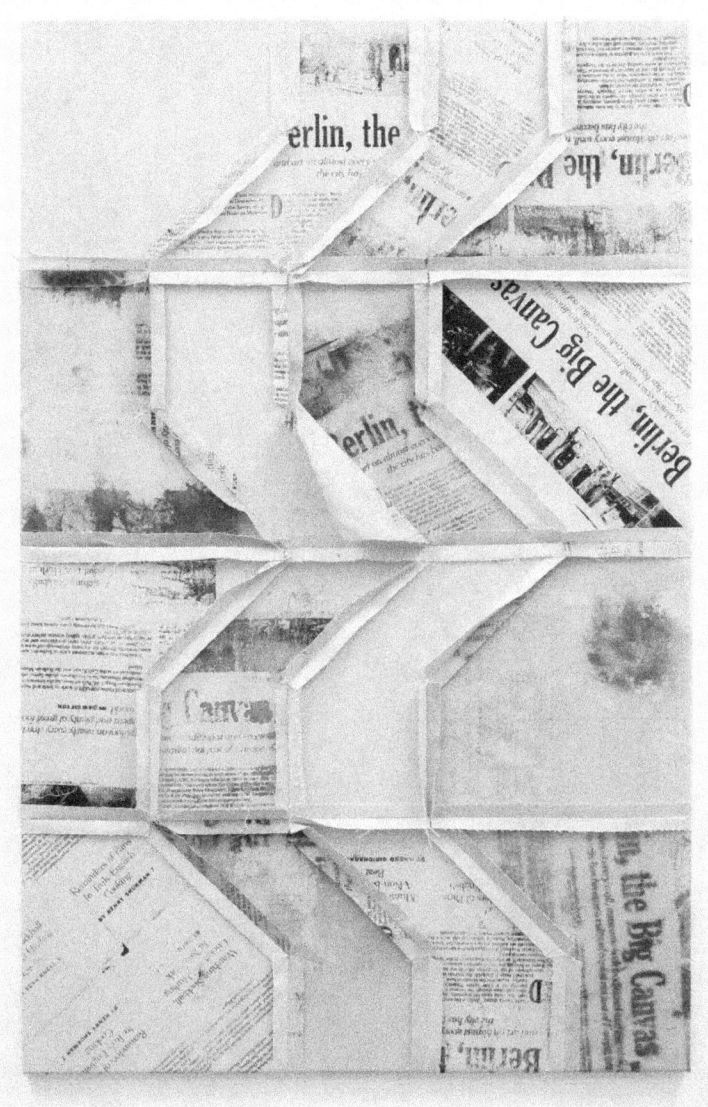

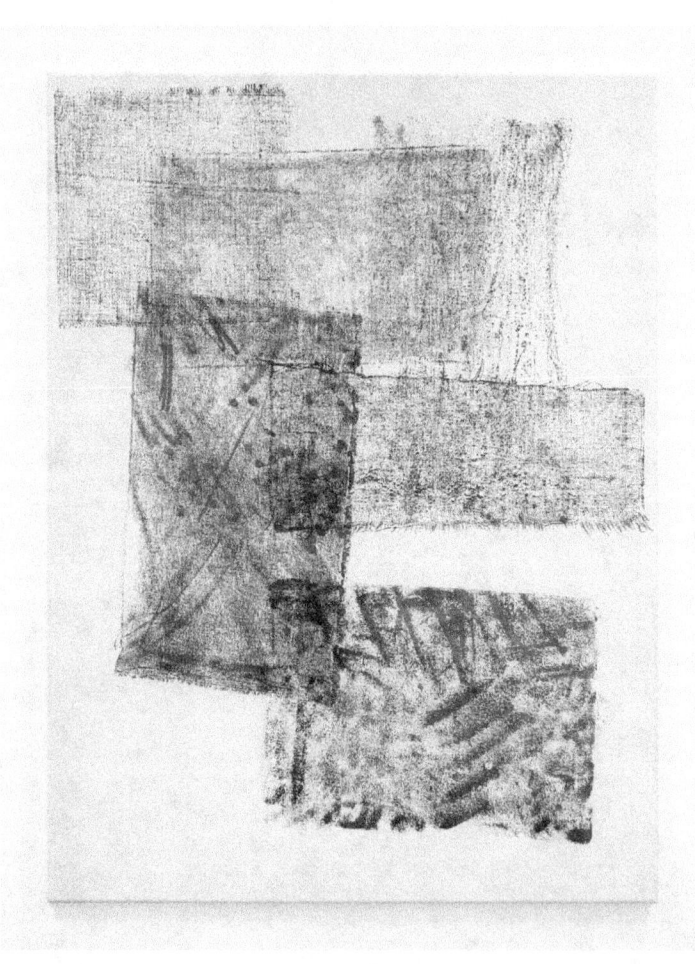

1   Untitled, 2001. Spray paint on canvas, 100 x 70cm
2   Untitled, 2001. Spray paint on canvas, 100 x 70cm
3   Untitled, 2001. Spray paint on canvas, 100 x 70cm
4   Untitled, 2001. Spray paint on canvas, 100 x 70cm
5   Untitled, 2001. Spray paint on canvas, 100 x 70cm
6   Untitled, 2001. Spray paint on canvas, 100 x 70cm
7   Untitled, 2001. Acrylic and spray paint on canvas, 100 x 70cm
8   Untitled, 2001. Acrylic and spray paint on canvas, 100 x 70cm
9   Untitled, 2001. Acrylic on canvas, 100 x 70cm
10   Untitled, 2001. Acrylic on canvas, 100 x 70cm
11   Untitled, 2001. Spray paint on canvas, 70 x 100cm
12   Untitled, 2002. Fabric and acrylic on canvas, 80 x 110cm
13   Untitled, 2002. Fabric and acrylic on canvas, 110 x 80cm
14   Untitled, 2002. Acrylic on canvas, 110 x 80cm
15   Untitled, 2002. Acrylic on canvas, 110 x 80cm
16   Untitled, 2002. Acrylic and marker on canvas, 110 x 80cm
17   Postcard Painting, 2002, Acrylic on canvas, 105 x 150cm
18   Untitled, 2002. Acrylic on fabric, 110 x 80cm
19   Untitled, 2002. Acrylic on fabric, 80 x 110cm
20   Untitled, 2002. Acrylic on canvas, 110 x 80cm
21   Untitled, 2003. Sewn canvas, thread, 120 x 90cm
22   Untitled, 2003. Sewn polyester tarps, 120 x 90cm
23   Untitled, 2003. Sewn plastic bags, 120 x 90cm
24   Untitled, 2003. Sewn plastic bags, 120 x 90cm
25   Untitled, 2003. Sewn polyester tarps and cotton, 120 x 90cm
26   Untitled, 2003. Acrylic on plastic bag and linen, 120 x 90cm
27   Postcard Painting, 2003, Acrylic on canvas, 105 x 150cm
28   Untitled, 2003. Acrylic on canvas, 120 x 90cm
29   Untitled, 2003. Spray paint on canvas, 120 x 90cm
30   Untitled, 2004. Spray paint on canvas, 130 x 100cm
31   Untitled, 2004. Acrylic on cotton, 137 x 110cm
32   Untitled, 2004. Enamel on plastic tarp, 130 x 100cm
33   Untitled, 2004. Enamel on plastic tarp, 130 x 100cm
34   Untitled, 2004. Acrylic on fabric, 130 x 100cm
35   Untitled, 2004. Torn paper on canvas, 110 x 80cm
36   Untitled, 2005. Sewn plastic bags, 140 x 110cm
37   Untitled, 2005. Acrylic, dirt, thread on canvas, 140 x 110cm
38   Untitled, 2005. Acrylic on fabric, 130 x 100cm
39   Untitled, 2005. Spray paint on canvas, 130 x 100cm
40   Untitled, 2005. Acrylic on fabric, 130 x 100cm
41   Untitled, 2005. Acrylic, emulsion, thread on canvas and linen, 130 x 100cm
42   Untitled, 2005. Acrylic on canvas and cotton, 120 x 90cm
43   Untitled, 2005. Acrylic on fabric and canvas, 130 x 100cm
44   Untitled, 2005. Sewn canvas, thread, 120 x 90cm
45   Untitled, 2006. Acrylic on canvas, 120 x 90cm
46   Untitled, 2006. Spray paint on canvas, 163 x 50cm
47   Untitled, 2006. Acrylic and spray paint on canvas, 119 x 91cm
48   Untitled, 2006. Acrylic and dirt on canvas, 100 x 100 cm
49   Untitled, 2006. Acrylic on fabric, 140 x 110cm
50   Untitled, 2006. Acrylic on canvas, 130 x 100cm
51   Untitled, 2006. Acrylic and dirt on canvas, 100 x 100cm

52   Untitled, 2006. Spray paint and emulsion on canvas, 110 x 80cm
53   Untitled, 2006. Acrylic on sewn canvas and fabric, 120 x 90cm
54   Untitled, 2006. Acrylic on fabric, wood frame, 145 x 95cm
55   Untitled, 2006. Acrylic on sewn canvas and linen, 120 x 90cm
56   Untitled, 2007. Acrylic and thread on sewn canvas, 110 x 80cm
57   Untitled, 2007. Acrylic, confetti and dirt on canvas, 100 x 100cm
58   Détournement, 2007. Acrylic on canvas, dyed canvas, buttons, 100 x 100cm (variable dimensions)
59   Détournement, 2007. Canvas, dyed canvas, buttons, 125 x 75cm (variable dimensions)
60   Détournement, 2007. Canvas, dyed canvas, buttons, 75 x 100cm (variable dimensions)
61   Aedicula Rahmen, 2007. Silkscreen and acrylic on canvas, 120 x 90cm
62   Untitled, 2007. Varnish on canvas, 120 x 90cm
63   Schmetterlinge II, 2007. Silkscreen and acrylic on canvas, 120 x 90 cm
64   Untitled, 2007. Sewn canvas and velvet, 200 x 200cm
65   Untitled, 2007. Acrylic on linen, 130 x 100cm
66   Untitled, 2007. Acrylic and fabric on canvas, 120 x 90cm
67   Détournement, 2007. Acrylic on canvas, buttons, 125 x 25cm (variable dimensions)
68   Untitled, 2007. Acrylic on canvas, 130 x 100cm
69   Untitled, 2007. Acrylic on canvas, dyed canvas, thread, 200 x 200cm
70   Untitled, 2007. Sewn dyed canvas, thread, 200 x 200cm
71   Untitled, 2007. Bleach on sewn denim, thread, 130 x 90cm
72   Détournement, 2008. Acrylic and oil on canvas, buttons, 100 x 130cm (variable dimensions)
73   Untitled, 2008. Acrylic on canvas, 120 x 90cm
74   Untitled, 2008. Acrylic on dyed canvas, 120 x 90cm
75   Untitled, 2008. Acrylic and spray paint on canvas, dyed canvas, 120 x 90cm
76   Untitled, 2008. Acrylic on sewn canvas, 135 x 90cm
77   Untitled, 2008. Woven denim and canvas, 120 x 90cm
78   Détournement, 2008. Acrylic and oil on canvas, buttons, 150 x 100cm (variable dimensions)
79   Untitled, 2008. Acrylic on sewn canvas and fabric, 150 x 105cm
80   Untitled, 2008. Oil on canvas sewn on cotton, 100 x 100cm
81   Untitled, 2008. Acrylic on sewn canvas and linen, 130 x 100cm
82   Untitled, 2008. Acrylic on sewn canvas and linen, 70 x 100cm
83   Untitled, 2008. Acrylic on sewn canvas and linen, 150 x 105cm
84   Détournement, 2007. Acrylic, spray paint on canvas and fabric, buttons, 150 x 100cm (variable dimensions)
85   Untitled, 2008. Acrylic on sewn canvas and linen, 120 x 90cm
86   Non Commodity, 2009. Dyed canvas, Velcro, 140 x 120cm (variable dimensions)
87   Untitled, 2009. Acrylic on sewn canvas and linen, 110 x 80cm
88   Untitled, 2009. Dyed canvas, 110 x 80cm
89   Untitled, 2009. Acrylic, spray paint on canvas and fabric, 120 x 90cm
90   Untitled, 2009. Primed canvas borders, 120 x 90cm
91   Non Commodity, 2009. Acrylic on canvas, Velcro, 250 x 100cm (variable dimensions)
92   Untitled, 2009. Acrylic and dirt on fabric, 120 x 90 cm
93   Untitled, 2009. Oil and acrylic on canvas and linen, 130 x 100cm
94   Untitled, 2009. Oil and acrylic on canvas and linen, 100 x 70cm
95   Untitled, 2009. Spray paint on canvas and fabric, 135 x 90cm
96   Untitled, 2009. Dyed canvas, 100 x 70cm
97   Untitled, 2009. Acrylic on canvas, fabric, woodchip wallpaper, 130 x 100cm
98   Untitled, 2009. Dyed canvas, 120 x 100cm
99   Untitled, 2009. Acrylic on sewn canvas and fabric, 125 x 85cm
100   Untitled, 2009. Emulsion on woodchip wallpaper on canvas, 120 x 90cm
101   Non Commodity, 2009. Acrylic on fabric, Velcro, 150 x 50cm (variable dimensions)
102   Untitled, 2009. Acrylic and oil on canvas and fabric, 130 x 90cm

103   Non Commodity, 2009. Acrylic on fabric and canvas, safety pins, 160 x 120cm (variable dimensions)

104   Untitled, 2009. Fabric and acrylic on canvas, 145 x 105cm

105   Untitled, 2010. Sewn dyed canvas, 220 x 160cm

106   Untitled, 2010. Acrylic on sewn canvas, 125 x 100cm

107   Untitled, 2010. Sewn dyed canvas, 200 x 200cm

108   Untitled, 2010. Sewn dyed canvas, 200 x 200cm

109   Untitled, 2010. Acrylic on canvas, 133 x 155cm

110   Untitled, 2010. Acrylic on canvas, fabric and linen, 150 x 105cm

111   Untitled, 2010. Dyed canvas and fabric, 210 x 100cm

112   Untitled, 2010. Acrylic on canvas and fabric, 140 x 100cm

113   Untitled, 2010. Dirt and acrylic on sewn canvas, 140 x 100cm

114   Untitled, 2010. Sewn dyed canvas, 180 x 105cm

115   Untitled, 2010. Sewn polyester tarp, 140 x 100cm

116   Untitled, 2010. Acrylic and thread on canvas and linen, 150 x 100cm

117   Untitled, 2010. Dyed canvas and tarp, 132 x 99cm

118   Untitled, 2010. Thread and sewn dyed canvas, 137 x 101cm

119   Untitled, 2010. Sewn dyed canvas, 119 x 102cm

120   Untitled, 2010. Acrylic and thread on canvas and linen, 136 x 90cm

121   Untitled, 2010. Sewn dyed canvas, 184 x 60cm

122   Untitled, 2010. Sewn dyed canvas and canvas, 142 x 107cm

123   Double Frame, 2011. Acrylic on canvas, plastic frame, wood frame, glass, 42 x 35cm

124   Untitled, 2011. Sewn dyed canvas, 189 x 114cm

125   Untitled, 2011. Sewn dyed canvas, 189 x 114cm

126   Untitled, 2011. Thread on sewn dyed canvas, 122 x 84cm

127   Untitled, 2011. Thread on sewn dyed canvas, 127 x 92cm

128   Untitled, 2011. Emulsion frottage on canvas, 110 x 77cm

129   Double Frame, 2011. Acrylic on wood, plastic frame, wood frame, glass, 42 x 35cm

130   Untitled, 2011. Emulsion frottage, xeroxes on fabric, 120 x 88cm

131   Untitled, 2011. Emulsion frottage, acrylic, xeroxes on fabric, 120 x 88cm

132   Edition for Westphalie, 2011. Silkscreen on paper, 42 x 30cm

133   Non Commodity, 2011. Silkscreen and woodblock print on drop cloth, Velcro, 110 x 50cm (variable dimensions)

134   Non Commodity, 2011. Silkscreen and woodblock print on drop cloth, Velcro, 90 x 80cm (variable dimensions)

135   Untitled, 2011. Fabric dye on sewn drop cloth, 145 x 97cm

136   Untitled, 2011. Thread on sewn dyed canvas, 145 x 97cm

137   Untitled, 2011. Fabric dye on sewn canvas, 137 x 91cm

138   Untitled, 2011. Woven dyed canvas, 145 x 97cm

139   Untitled, 2011. Fabric dye on sewn canvas, 145 x 97cm

140   Untitled, 2011. Fabric dye on sewn canvas, 148 x 109cm

141   Untitled, 2011. Fabric dye on sewn drop cloth, 152 x 102cm

142   Untitled, 2011. Silkscreen on sewn canvas, 145 x 97cm

143   Untitled, 2011. Sewn dyed canvas, 145 x 97cm

144   Untitled, 2011. Fabric dye on sewn canvas, 145 x 109cm

145   Untitled, 2012. Silkscreen on sewn drop cloth, 145 x 97cm

146   Untitled, 2011. Silkscreen on sewn canvas and drop cloth, 137 x 91cm

147   Untitled, 2012. Silkscreen on sewn drop cloth, 145 x 97cm

148   Untitled, 2012. Fabric dye on sewn canvas, 145 x 97cm

149   Untitled, 2012. Fabric dye on sewn canvas, 145 x 110cm

149   Untitled, 2012. Silkscreen on sewn canvas, drop cloth, polyester tarp, 137 x 91cm

150   Untitled, 2012. Silkscreen on sewn canvas, 140 x 88cm

152   Untitled, 2012. Acrylic on canvas, 110 x 80cm

www.ingramcontent.com/pod-product-compliance
Lightning Source LLC
Chambersburg PA
CBHW060854170526
45158CB00001B/352